take a closer look

for women

take a closer look

for women

Uncommon and Unexpected Insights
to Inspire Every Area of Your Life

Jan Kern

HOWARD BOOKS

A DIVISION OF SIMON & SCHUSTER

New York   London   Toronto   Sydney

Our purpose at Howard Books is to:
· *Increase faith* in the hearts of growing Christians
· *Inspire holiness* in the lives of believers
· *Instill hope* in the hearts of struggling people everywhere
Because He's coming again!

HOWARD
BOOKS

Published by Howard Books, a division of Simon & Schuster, Inc.
1230 Avenue of the Americas, New York, NY 10020
www.howardpublishing.com

Take a Closer Look for Women © 2007 by GRQ, Inc.

ISBN-13: 978-1-4165-4215-5
ISBN 10:   1-4165-4215-9
ISBN 13: 978-1-58229-684-5 (gift edition)
ISBN 10:   1-58229-684-7 (gift edition)

10 9 8 7 6 5 4 3 2 1

For information regarding special discounts for bulk purchases, please contact: Simon & Schuster Special Sales at 1-800-456-6798 or business@simonandschuster.com.

Managing Editor: Lila Empson
Associate Editor: Chrys Howard
Assistant Editor: Raelene Searle
Design: Whisner Design Group

Permissions for What Others Have Said:

Who may ascend into the hill of the Lord?
Or who may stand in His holy place?
He who has clean hands and a pure heart,
Who has not lifted up his soul to an idol,
Nor sworn deceitfully.
He shall receive blessing from the Lord,
And righteousness from the God of his salvation.
This is Jacob, the generation
of those who seek Him,
Who seek Your face.

Psalm 24:3–6 NKJV

Contents

Introduction

Perhaps you've held a piece of heirloom china, run your hand over the curves and the intricate design, and wondered about its history. Maybe the china had sat in your family's china cabinet for years, but then you were curious about it. You brought it out for a closer look. New questions stirred. Who first chose the treasured keepsake? Was it used only on special occasions? What happened to cause the tiny chip? The more you spent time getting to know the piece and its story, the more precious it became to you.

The stories of the Bible are like that. What you know about them has been passed down to you by pastors, teachers, or family members. Some stories you easily recognize; you know every twist and turn, and you know the endings. This book takes these stories—the familiar ones as well as a few less known—and brings them out for another look, a closer look.

Explore the stories, and you'll soon notice the Bible's use of Hebrew and Greek. Words were chosen by the original writers to give beautifully inspired shades of meaning to the text. John, one of Jesus' disciples, used several Greek words for forms of "to see" in his writing. In one verse he spoke of seeing the splendor and perfection of Jesus, whom God sent to live among them (John 1:14). He used the Greek word *theaomai*, which means "to take a closer look, to reflect on with amazement."

The following pages offer an opportunity for you to run your mind and heart over some of the intricacies of God's history and teachings in the Bible. Allow yourself to grow curious and take a closer look, then to reflect on what you find with wonder and enjoyment. As you spend time in these stories, may you discover how precious they are and how precious you are to God.

Robert C. Chapman

There are mysteries of grace and love in every page of the Bible; it is a thriving soul that finds the Book of God growing more and more precious.

Moses, not believing his eyes, went up to take a closer look. He heard God's voice.

Acts 7:31 MSG

J. I. Packer

Not until we have become humble and teachable, standing in awe of God's holiness and sovereignty . . . acknowledging our own littleness, distrusting our own thoughts, and willing to have our minds turned upside down, can divine wisdom become ours.

Humble yourselves, therefore, under the mighty hand of God so that at the proper time he may exalt you.

1 Peter 5:6 ESV

I Really Want to Know

The Spirit said to Philip, "Go over and join this chariot." So Philip ran to him and heard him reading Isaiah the prophet and asked, "Do you understand what you are reading?" And he said, "How can I, unless someone guides me?" And he invited Philip to come up and sit with him.

Acts 8:29–31 ESV

The Big Picture

Picture those places where you might chat with someone about God: a garden path or a coffee shop, places that are comfortable and away from distractions. But sometimes God has other plans—like the plan for Philip to go to the desert to talk to a man who was riding in a chariot.

In the book of Acts, Philip was one of seven selected to help Jesus' apostles. A Greek-speaking Jew, he at first focused his work on the care of the Greek widows and the poor people who were part of the Christian church in Jerusalem. This new church was blossoming. Those who witnessed Jesus' powerful life, death, and resurrection shared their message of hope about Jesus the Messiah. Many responded. But during that time the religious leaders intensified their persecution of Christians. As more friends and family were killed or scattered, Philip's duties shifted to that of an evangelist. He spoke boldly about Jesus, and many listened.

Philip had been speaking in the villages of Samaria, north of Jerusalem. When he returned, he received a very specific order from one of God's angels:

"Go south along the desert road that goes from Jerusalem to Gaza." Philip had no idea *why* he was to go, but the Bible says he arose and went.

Traveling through the parched land, Philip saw a man riding in a chariot. He was a eunuch in office, highly respected and trusted in his position as treasurer for the queen of Ethiopia. He had gone to worship in Jerusalem and was on his way home. While he rode in the chariot, he puzzled over the words in the Bible of Isaiah the prophet.

Philip, directed by God's Spirit, ran alongside the chariot. "Do you understand what you're reading?" he asked the Ethiopian man.

The man looked up. "How can I without an explanation?" So urgent was his desire to understand, he invited Philip to join him and tell him what it meant.

While the chariot moved along, Philip and the man pored over the ancient words that foretold Jesus' life and death. God's Spirit worked to bring understanding to the Ethiopian. When the chariot came to a river, the man was so thoroughly convinced of Jesus' identity that he asked to be baptized.

Philip was in the right place at the right time, ready to help someone understand the truth about Jesus.

I love those who love me, and those who seek me diligently will find me.

Proverbs 8:17 NKJV

The Ethiopian man really wanted to know the truth about Jesus. Look closely and you see that his searching had begun before God's angel directed Philip to the Gaza desert to meet him.

Ethiopia was, and still is, about fifteen hundred miles away from Jerusalem. Those are a lot of bumpy miles along dusty desert roads to get to Jerusalem to worship. Why all that way? It's possible that centuries before, Judaism had spread to Ethiopia after royalty from that country visited Jerusalem. The Ethiopian man might have had Jewish roots and desired to travel to Jerusalem to attend an important feast.

Regardless, it's clear that the man's trip was more than mere duty. On his way home, he had questions and didn't mind asking for answers. He hungered to understand. That day in the chariot, his interest focused on a few sentences that Isaiah had written. These spoke about someone's unjust humiliation and death. The Ethiopian knew it was a prophecy and considered the source reliable. He questioned who it could be that was led like a "lamb to the slaughter." Philip told him it was Jesus. The Ethiopian, who really wanted to know the truth, was ready to believe.

> *God is always previous. God is always there first, and if you have any desire for God and for the things of God, it is God himself who put it there.*
>
> A. W. Tozer

Picture Philip and the Ethiopian traveling along in the chariot—heads bent down in intense discussion over the words of Isaiah while the horses trotted down the road. God was there too. He orchestrated the whole event. He does that.

He knew the Ethiopian's hunger to accurately know the truth about him. He knew of his persistence—that he was willing to go whatever distance it took and that he was willing to ask the questions that plagued his heart.

Picture yourself with a friend chatting at your kitchen table over a favorite cup of tea, discussing the questions that plague your heart. God is just as present in your conversation as he was in Philip's and the Ethiopian's. And like the eunuch, your questions about the words you read in the Bible will be answered.

Take advantage of the richness of the wisdom of other women who have gone before you in asking the deeper questions about God, those who have studied the words of the Bible longer. You won't ever understand it all, but know as you and your friend sit with your heads bent together, searching, that God is there also. He will help you find the answers you long for.

Deal with Your servant according to Your lovingkindness and teach me Your statutes. I am Your servant; give me understanding, that I may know Your testimonies.

Psalm 119:124–125 NASB

The Ethiopian man is a wonderful example of someone who was grateful for those who could help him understand the Bible. John Gill, in *John Gill's Exposition of the Entire Bible*, said:

"Instead of charging Philip with impertinence and insolence in interrupting him whilst reading, and putting such a question to him, he expresses himself with great and uncommon modesty, with a sense and confession of his ignorance and incapacity and of the necessity and usefulness of the instructions of men, appointed of God to open and explain the Scriptures."

David Guzik encouraged people to welcome the teaching of others. In his Enduring Word Commentary series, he said:

"It was good for the Ethiopian to be reading the Bible, but unless understanding was brought to him, there would be little benefit from his reading. But God had brought someone (Philip) to bring understanding. . . . How can I, unless someone guides me? This is the proper question of anyone who wants to understand the Bible. We should never feel bad if we need to be taught before we understand many things."

Zooming In

Eunuch comes from the Greek word *eunouchos* and literally means "a keeper of the bed." The term often referred to a castrated male employed to take charge of the women of a royal household. It also can be used to describe a person of quality and dignity who is trusted and given an office of great authority.

The Old Testament records the visit of Queen Sheba to King Solomon in Jerusalem. According to Ethiopian tradition she took Judaism as her own religion, and it spread in Ethiopia. Some historians say that she had a child by Solomon, presumably the beginning of the race of black Ethiopian Jews called *Falashas* who practiced a less-orthodox form of Judaism.

The Ethiopian man yearned to understand more about God. You can pray for the same thing. When you do, you'll find God meeting you in new and deeper ways.

It can be embarrassing to admit you don't understand something. Do you have a friend you feel is safe, to whom you can go to for answers to your questions about God?

_____

_____

_____

_____

Make learning about God delightful. What favorite places could be your "chariot" where you can invite a friend to join you?

_____

_____

_____

Are you a Philip, too? Whom do you know who needs a friend to come alongside her on the dusty roads in life? How might you encourage her?

_____

_____

Words You Can Trust

"Nothing, you see, is impossible with God." And Mary said, "Yes, I see it all now: I'm the Lord's maid, ready to serve. Let it be with me just as you say." Then the angel left her.

Luke 1:37–38 MSG

The Big Picture

Mary was a young woman engaged to be married to a man named Joseph. What excitement must have filled her heart as she prepared and waited for her wedding day. Of course little snags might occur as they do in any plans for a big event. But when that angel showed up, his news presented more than a simple snag.

First of all, an angel appearing in front of you wasn't an everyday occurrence. And this wasn't just any nameless angel. It was Gabriel, sent from God specifically to address Mary, who lived in Nazareth, a city of the region of Galilee. And not just any Mary in Nazareth, but the one who was a virgin engaged to Joseph, of the house of David. *That* Mary.

Gabriel addressed her with honor. He told her she was highly favored and blessed and the Lord was with her. Good words—wonderfully complimentary—but wouldn't you wonder, as Mary did, what was up? She was startled by the angel's appearance and perplexed by his greeting. Gabriel calmed her before he broke the really crazy news: She would become pregnant and give birth to a son whom she would name Jesus. He would be great, and God would give him the throne of his father David. He would reign over the house of Jacob, and his kingdom would never end.

This must have sounded amazing to Mary. Her people had been waiting for the promised Messiah for centuries. She would be his mother? But it didn't make sense. How would this happen? She was a virgin. The angel explained how God would make it happen and the holy one to be born would be God's Son. Perhaps to remind her how the impossible could truly happen, he told her about her much older cousin, Elizabeth, who couldn't have children. She was now six months pregnant. "Nothing," the angel assured Mary, "is impossible with God."

At that point, Mary saw that it was all true and willingly submitted to what was to be. She told him, "I am the Lord's servant. Let it be as you have said."

What incredible news this must have been to this young woman. In just a few moments her view of her life was changed forever. She was to be a part of God's plan to bring the Messiah—the one whom the Jews had been waiting for.

I have found that there are three stages in every great work of God: first, it is impossible, then it is difficult, then it is done.

Hudson Taylor

Gabriel's announcement shows God's consistency in bringing about all his plans. A closer look reveals the strength and certainty of the angel's promise when he told Mary that nothing is impossible with God.

Growing up in the Jewish tradition, Mary was familiar with the writings of the Old Testament and the prophecies of the coming Messiah. Her question "How could this be?" was not doubt of God's ability or character, but an understandable inquiry into how a virgin could possibly give birth.

As part of his reply, the angel informed her of Elizabeth's pregnancy. Mary knew of Jewish ancestors to whom God had miraculously given the gift of a child. Elizabeth, too? With that established, the angel told her that nothing is impossible with God.

What is not often interpreted from the Greek in that statement is *rhema*, meaning "word." Further, *pas*, the word for "nothing," can be translated "not one." The angel told Mary that not one word God has said can be void of power.

Mary, confident of the history of God's consistency, now applied that assurance to the announcement given to her by the angel. Without a doubt, she would be Jesus' mother.

Faith sees the invisible, believes the unbelievable, and receives the impossible.

Corrie ten Boom

The Bible is full of God's assurances, but each day can bring challenges to your belief that he will follow through and meet you in the impossible circumstances.

Apply It to Your Life

Perhaps you're caring for a loved one who is seriously ill while other responsibilities and relationships beg for your attention. You long for the escape of a soothing bath or a cappuccino that hasn't grown cold, but there isn't even time for that.

God knows all about what you are facing this week, and he cares. Think about what you know is true about him. He is powerful. He is consistent. That applies to his words and his actions: What he says, he will do—powerfully.

Now trust his words and put yourself into God's loving arms. Mary did. Say as she did, "I am your daughter who longs to serve you. I trust your words. Do your work, for I have confidence that it is good."

Here are two of God's powerful assurances from the Bible: He will be with you, and he will not leave you. Believe them. They're for you.

What is impossible with men is possible with God.
Luke 18:27 NIV

A prayer that believes in the impossible focuses on faith in a powerful God. A. W. Tozer, in *Believing Prayer*, said:

"Whatever God can do, faith can do; and whatever faith can do, prayer can do when it is offered in faith. An invitation to prayer is, therefore, an invitation to omnipotence, for prayer engages the Omnipotent God and brings Him into our human affairs. Nothing is impossible to the Christian who prays in faith, just as nothing is impossible with God."

C. H. Mackintosh felt that the impossible won't faze the one who prays in faith. In *Notes on the Pentateuch* he said:

"Faith says, 'If "impossible" is the only objection, it can be done!' Faith brings God into the scene, and therefore it knows absolutely nothing of difficulties—it laughs at impossibilities. . . . Unbelief says, 'How can such and such things be?' It is full of 'Hows'; but faith has one great answer to ten thousand 'hows,' and that answer is—God."

Zooming **In**

A betrothal in Mary's time was considered the beginning of the union between a man and a woman. It became legally binding when the man, or his messenger, handed the woman a small amount of money or a letter stating his intentions. This was done before witnesses and then couldn't be dissolved except by divorce.

Today's use of a bridal veil dates back to ancient times. A Jewish bride wore her hair loose but carefully covered her head and hair with a veil. The veil was a symbol of the woman's modesty and virtue. One very ancient belief was that evil spirits could gain power over a woman whose head was uncovered.

God is aware of the weight of your present circumstance. Let him carry it for you. Let him show you his limitless capacity to meet the impossible.

When you're worn out, it's easy to begin to think God can't help you. What is one way you can take time to rest so you can renew your perspective?

_____

_____

_____

_____

God cared about Mary's concerns, questions, and feelings. He cares about yours, too. Write a note to God about your impossible situation. What might he tell you in response?

_____

_____

_____

God is consistent. His words are powerful. What he has said, he will do. These are trust reminders. What reminders will help you place the "impossible" in the realm of the "possible"?

_____

_____

_____

Hiding from Love

Toward evening they heard the LORD God walking about in the garden, so they hid themselves among the trees. The LORD God called to Adam, "Where are you?" He replied, "I heard you, so I hid. I was afraid because I was naked."

Genesis 3:8–10 NLT

The Big Picture

From the beginning of time people have been hiding from God in one way or another. Amazing—the created hiding from the Creator.

Out of nothing God created. Each of the six days of his loving labor and design brought something completely new, magnificent, and alive. On the last day God created Adam. He made him the keeper of a garden in Eden and told him, "Eat and enjoy the fruit of every tree in this garden, but not the fruit from the tree of knowledge of good and evil. You will surely die the day you eat from that tree." That same day God also made a companion for Adam. Her name was Eve. He created both *in his image*. What an honor.

And then God rested.

No one knows how much time lapsed between that seventh day—the day of rest—and what came next. It might have been the following day that the serpent visited the garden. His name? Satan. He had once been a glorious angel created to worship God. Instead he craved to be worshipped above

God. Pride consumed him. He revolted and became God's vilest adversary. On that day in the garden, Satan launched his plan to strengthen his rebellion and destroy God's most beloved creation—mankind.

Eve was alone. The serpent cunningly lured her with questions and lies that implied God was not to be trusted. *Why obey him? Every tree but one? God holds back the best from you. Eat the fruit. You won't die. You'll become as gods, knowing good and evil. Don't you want to be wise?*

The fruit grew appealing to Eve. She ate it and encouraged Adam to do the same. *Snap.* The trap had sprung. At that moment innocence died. Adam and Eve realized they were naked, and that, for the first time, was shameful. They twisted giant leaves around themselves. The foliage worked for their bodies, but not their souls.

When God walked through the garden toward them, Adam and Eve hid among the trees in fear. In answer to God's call, Adam cried out, "I heard you, but I was afraid. I am naked." God questioned him as to who told him he was naked, and if they had eaten from the tree. Did they disobey him? He knew they had. They knew it was wrong. Adam pointed to Eve. Eve said the serpent tricked her. Behind blame, the created hid from the Creator.

Leave the broken, irreversible past in God's hands, and step out into the invincible future with Him.

Oswald Chambers

You see a lot of hiding and covering up going on in this story. Satan approached Eve first. Imagine her shame as she hid. Imagine her fear of punishment, possibly death. A closer look reveals that God came to restore the broken relationship. Eve didn't know it yet, but she was hiding from love.

In Eve's reaction to hide from God with Adam, you see characteristics of an established relationship. She knew it was God walking in the garden. When God called out, she recognized his voice. Even more, she knew they had disobeyed God. That mattered to her.

On God's side of things, you see his pursuit. Yes, there would be consequences for Eve and Adam's actions—many in fact. But at that moment, he came in the cool of the day, the calm of the evening. He didn't charge into the garden; he walked. Though he knew where his beloved ones hid, he called out, "Where are you?" and gave them an opportunity to answer. In her nakedness and shame, could Eve respond with Adam, "I am here"? Could she come out of hiding? When she finally did, she found God still wanted to love her.

God loves each of us as if there were only one of us.

Saint Augustine

It's amazing what shame can do to you. It skews your perspective and convinces you that you're disappointing and irreconcilably bad. That kind of shame feels so awful, you feel you have to hide.

Apply It
to Your Life

It could be that the same enemy who distorted the truth, and lured Eve, may be whispering lies to you: *Look at what you've done. See how you've hurt people, disappointed many. You're weak. You're worthless. Who needs you? Even God doesn't want you.*

This enemy would be delighted if you gave up. From the beginning, he has plotted to destroy God's design of you as a woman. He would be happy to convince you that you are hopelessly caught in the snares of your shame.

But you are not. Listen as God softly walks toward you, calling, "Where are you?" He pursues you in love. Hear him? *What have you done, my daughter, my beloved? Come, receive mercy and healing. You are worth everything to me. I cannot lose you.*

No matter what you've done, it won't stop him from seeking out a healing relationship with you. Shame is powerful, but it doesn't have to keep you in hiding.

Whenever we are in need, we should come bravely before the throne of our merciful God. There we will be treated with undeserved kindness, and we will find help.

Hebrews 4:16 CEV

God's anger and love at the moment of Adam and Eve's disobedience are not in opposition to one another. In his book *The God Who Loves,* John MacArthur addressed this:

"His wrath is not inconsistent with His love. Because He so completely loves what is true and right, He must hate all that is false and wrong. Because He so perfectly loves His children, He seeks what blesses and edifies them, and hates all that curses and debases them. Therefore, His wrath against sin is actually an expression of His love for His people."

Matthew Henry, in *Matthew Henry's Commentary of the Whole Bible,* called God's question "Where are you?" a "gracious pursuit." What he said of Adam also applied to Eve:

"If God had not called to him, to reclaim him, his condition would have been as desperate as that of fallen angels; this lost sheep would have wandered endlessly, if the good Shepherd had not sought after him, to bring him back, and, in order to that, reminded him where he was, where he should not be, and where he could not be either happy or easy."

Zooming In

The Hebrew word used for the type of leaves Adam and Eve used to cover themselves is *te'enah*, meaning "fig." Some say the leaves came from a tree similar to an Indian fig, under which fifty horsemen might find shade away from a noonday sun. The span of these leaves is said to be that of an Amazonian shield.

The location of the mysterious Garden of Eden has been investigated since ancient times. Two of its four rivers are still in existence today—the Tigris and the Euphrates. The other two are entirely unknown, even in ancient history. Current thought is that the garden might be buried within what is now the Persian Gulf.

You are a woman of God's design. God comes to you with his love, calling you out of hiding, calling you to himself.

Through the
Eyes of
Your Heart

What are some of the lies you have believed that are keeping you bound in shame? As a woman created in God's image, what truths can you believe instead?

_____

_____

_____

Sit in a cool garden and imagine God calling, "Where are you?" Are there ways you are afraid of him?

_____

_____

_____

_____

"I am here" is a responsive step out of hiding. Can you trust God to love you out of shame, bringing you back into relationship with him?

_____

_____

_____

_____

An Endless Gift

The woman said, "I am surprised that you ask me for a drink, since you are a Jewish man and I am a Samaritan woman." (Jewish people are not friends with Samaritans.) Jesus said, "If you only knew the free gift of God and who it is that is asking you for water, you would have asked him, and he would have given you living water."

John 4:9–10 NCV

The Big Picture

Weariness of life parches the soul. Every footstep through the day feels increasingly heavy and difficult. Whether from circumstances or regretted choices, the Samaritan woman might have felt that way as she traveled to the well.

The well sat outside the town of Sychar in Samaria. Though nearer sources of water existed, it was better to get her water farther away, and when the sun was high in the sky. The other Samaritan women wouldn't fetch water at that time. No one would sneer at her and whisper behind her back: *There's that wretched woman who has had many husbands. Stay away from her.*

As she worked her way along the road, she might have passed twelve Jewish men traveling toward town to purchase that day's provisions. She wouldn't speak to them. They'd never speak to her. She was a Samaritan. Jews had a long-standing feud with the Samaritans, seeing them as a mixed breed, cursed, and not fit to live. Just being a woman, the men might avoid her—especially her.

Jesus sat at the side of the well waiting. He'd be there until the disciples returned with their purchases. But before they came back, he'd be there for the Samaritan woman.

She arrived carrying her empty water pot and noticed the stranger—*another Jew*—sitting by the well. She would get her water and leave.

"Could I have a drink?" he asked.

Startled, she turned to him. "You're a Jew. Why is it that you're asking me, a Samaritan woman, for a drink? Jews don't want anything to do with Samaritans."

Instead of reacting to her defensive reply, with compassion he told her something even more mystifying: "If you understood the gift of God, and who it is who is asking you for water, you would have asked him for living water."

She then challenged him on two accounts: the impossibility of drawing flowing water from the deep well, and how he could claim to be greater than Jacob, their honored ancestor who built the well.

In the next moments, Jesus led the Samaritan woman on a journey of revelation. This man knew the awful secrets of her life. He challenged her to live differently. She would discover that he was the Messiah. The gift of living water was his everlasting mercy. It was a different kind of water. With his water, she'd never be thirsty in her soul again.

Blessed are those who hunger and thirst for righteousness, for they shall be filled.

Matthew 5:6 NKJV

The woman was surprised that Jesus ignored the prejudices of his Jewish culture. But notice, absolutely nothing of what happened surprised Jesus. He arrived in Samaria with a determined plan to give a gift, and he would begin with a particular woman at a well.

Jesus had never met this woman, but he knew all about her. He knew her heart. His words were filled with compassion as he spoke specifically to her beliefs and her life. He knew what traditions mattered to her, and how she worshipped and lived. He used a picture snapped from the toil of her daily existence: the real condition of thirst, and the drudgery of going for water every day. He turned that into an offer for living water.

He carefully laid bare all that would keep her from this living water—a hardness, a belief, a lie. Each revelation freed her a little more. And then he shared another that would free her forever: "I am the Messiah you have waited for. The grace I give is like living water that never stops flowing."

The Samaritan woman came to the well, alone, with an empty water pot and an empty life. Jesus gave her a gift that never ends, and she walked away full.

> As rivers, the nearer they come to the ocean whither they tend, the more they increase their waters, and speed their streams; so will grace flow more fully and freely in its near approaches to the ocean of glory.
>
> John Owen

A difficult past can dim the present. Even if you feel as if you're a different person today, memories and regrets cast their long shadows. Labels, either others' or your own, are hard to shake. You begin to believe them after a while.

Apply It to Your Life

The Samaritan woman might have felt that way, too. She went to the well alone. Her choices and circumstances made her an outcast, but she probably hoped her life would get better. Jesus took the time with her, alone, and carefully showed her who he was and who she could become. She could be freed from her past.

Jesus knows you as well as he knew the Samaritan woman—every detail, every hurt, every mistake. He knows your toil. He knows your loneliness. You have sat by your well of hurts day after day, but now he offers you his living water. Take it. Let it wash away the labels, memories, and regrets—forever.

Now see yourself as he sees you. You are beautiful. You are loved. You are forgiven.

Remember these truths the next time you are discouraged by the shadows of your past. Remember that Jesus comes to you personally, to encourage you toward all you can become. Spend time at his well.

O God, you are my God, earnestly I seek you; my soul thirsts for you, my body longs for you, in a dry and weary land where there is no water.

Psalm 63:1 NIV

The story highlights the interaction between an individual and Jesus. The result was a dramatic change of heart. J. Alexander Findlay, in *The Fourth Gospel*, said:

"Jesus came to the fountain as a hunter. . . . He threw a grain before one pigeon that He might catch the whole flock. . . . She tried to get the better of the thirsty man, she showed her dislike of the Jew, she heckled the Rabbi, she was swept off her feet by the prophet, and she adored the Christ."

Brent Riggs, author of Daily Devotions at seriousfaith.com, warned about the wrong places to quench your thirst:

"We all thirst. It's part of our nature. We thirst for happiness. We thirst for love. We thirst for fulfillment. We thirst for contentment. We thirst for completion. And we thirst for restoration. . . . The world claims to quench your thirst with materialism, pleasure, drugs, achievement, or recreation. Oh, it does quench your thirst temporarily. But like the sun rising in the east, it will return like clockwork. Jesus offers the drink which quenches, satisfies, and fills."

Zooming **In**

"Living water" was a common expression in ancient times, and referred to water that flowed, like that from streams, rivers, and fountains. These waters were called "living" because they continued to flow rather than grow stagnant. Traditionally, rabbis have used water that flowed for ritual purification.

For more than twenty-three centuries, Samaritans have believed the well mentioned in John 4 was the one built by the Jacob of the book of Genesis. Such a well still exists today near Sychar. An explorer in AD 670 said it was 240 feet deep. In 1861 it was reported to be only 75 feet deep.

Jesus comes to sit at your well, and offers an endless gift—his Spirit living inside you. He comes to you—personally—knowing all that might keep you from enjoying his gift.

Through the
Eyes of
Your Heart

What do you find in your well of regrets and hurts? What do you long for instead? Will it free you?

_____

_____

_____

_____

Jesus sees the beautiful person you can be, not the labels you're hanging on to. When you shed those, what do you see?

_____

_____

_____

_____

Are there loved ones you have hurt? Each request for forgiveness can bury one of your regrets. What might you do or say?

_____

_____

_____

_____

Perplexed and at Peace

He who observes the wind will not sow, and he who regards the clouds will not reap. As you do not know what is the way of the wind, or how the bones grow in the womb of her who is with child, so you do not know the works of God who makes everything.

Ecclesiastes 11:4–5 NKJV

The Big Picture

In the early days of his reign, Solomon dedicated his kingdom to God and sought his wisdom. At a place called Gibeon, God asked Solomon, in a dream, to name what he wanted to receive. Solomon humbly asked for understanding and discernment. God replied, "I will give you a wise and discerning mind." Further, because he had not asked for them, God gave Solomon unmatched riches and honor. He made one request: remain faithful—keep my commandments.

King Solomon demonstrated his wisdom through the administration of his kingdom and the execution of God's plans to build the temple in Jerusalem. He studied sciences and wrote proverbs and songs. He was renowned for his insightful judgments. But then he began to grapple with the possibilities of wealth, honor, possessions, and pleasure. After much extravagant living, he set out to study the meaning of life. He wrote a book, which was his way of gathering his listeners to tell them, "Behold, this is what I've found."

take a CLOSER look for women

At times, his Ecclesiastic proverbs poured lightly from his pen, but his discourses were heavy with reminders of the futility of his pursuits. He had concluded that riches and honors were meaningless, like "chasing after the wind." They could be good, possibly, if one were blessed by God.

He then told his listeners how they could make the most of their life in this meaningless world. He said the future was uncertain, and since gathering riches was meaningless, they would do well to share their abundance. He also advised them to be diligent in all they did. For the latter, he turned to the images of wind and rain. Both were inevitable, and beyond anyone's control. Since that was the case, he encouraged his listeners to be diligent and to work hard. Beyond anyone's comprehension were God's mysteries, like patterns of the wind, or how a baby develops in the womb. He advised that these mysteries not be deterrents to their diligence either.

King Solomon then spoke briefly to his younger listeners. He concluded by saying that wisdom itself was profound and difficult to discern. Even more, God's ways were complex, and much would remain a mystery. So, at the end of his searching, the king reached back to the directive once given in a dream: Fear God and keep his commandments. Living this out, he said, was what mattered most.

Earth's crammed with heaven, and every common bush afire with God; but only he who sees, takes off his shoes—the rest sit round it and pluck blackberries.

Elizabeth Barrett Browning

"A chasing after the wind" was one of Solomon's most repeated descriptions of the futility of pursuing anything apart from God. But in one place he said, "You don't know the way of the wind." This offered an important picture for Solomon. It was as if he was saying, "Take a moment to look at the elusive wind another way. See how it shows the great mystery of God's ways."

Solomon paired the way of the wind with the wonder of how a baby is formed in the womb. At that time, these were two entirely hidden and unobservable events. Meteorologists weren't appearing on nightly newscasts to explain wind patterns. Doctors, with intricate instruments, didn't provide pictures of a baby's first days in the womb. These were, and in many ways still are, extraordinary mysteries.

Solomon used these wonders to illustrate that no person can control the mysteries and plans of God—ever. He didn't want his readers to waste their time, as he felt he had, trying to understand. Instead, through wonders like the wind, he showed them that God and his ways were too big to grasp, and that was okay. They could be at peace, and get back to making the most of their time.

> *Mystery is not the absence of meaning, but the presence of more meaning than we can comprehend.*
>
> Dennis Covington

Wind. It has retained its mystery, but is considered more of an "everyday" wonder. Except for your local meteorologist, there likely aren't many you know who contemplate its intricacies. You, on the other hand, might have more pressing questions on your mind: the practical mysteries of the ways of God in the activities of your day, or simply in you.

Apply It
to Your Life

Think for a moment about what bothers you regarding the way God works. He can seem quite confusing. Solomon's lessons of the wind can help. He was right—that blustery invisible air that tangles your hair, or topples your potted plants, is elusive and incomprehensible. You can't put your hands on it. Just when you think you've figured out where it is, it moves. It can't be controlled. Wind, like all the rest of God's wonders, explodes the boundaries of your wisdom.

But here is where you begin to catch a glimpse of the largeness of God. Instead of being frustrated by the limits of your understanding, you bask in the wonder of the mysteries. The beyond-you-ness of your questions brings peace to the not-knowing-all-the-answers. The one who does know is in control, and he is big.

Look up at the sky! Who created the stars you see? The one who leads them out like an army, he knows how many there are and calls each one my name! His power is so great—not one of them is ever missing!

Isaiah 40:26 GNT

Janet Chester Bly encouraged a wider view of wonder in *Awakening Your Sense of Wonder: Discovering God in the Ordinary.* Here's what she said:

"Wonder is more than novelty. It's more than thrill-seeking, although it can appear as a sudden intrusion or invigorating jolt. The merely novel, the brief thrill is totally self-centered, what makes us feel good or superior. Wonder is deeper, wider, and healthier. Wonder is bumping up against an astounding world of external glory, then reverently entering in."

In *Dangerous Wonder: The Adventure of Childlike Faith*, Michael Yaconelli challenged readers to revive their weakened childlike wonder:

"We have lost the gleam in our eye. Jesus no longer chases us in the ragged terrain of our souls. We have forgotten what it is like to stand speechless in the presence of Jesus, hearts beating wildly, staggered and stunned by what God is doing in our world. . . . We can rediscover the childlike attribute of our faith called dangerous wonder."

Zooming **In**

Today some are saying that King Solomon never lived, but archaeologists are proving differently. The Bible tells about a time when an Egyptian pharaoh destroyed the city of Gezer. Solomon rebuilt Gezer, and then also began extensive building projects in Jerusalem, Hazor, and Megiddo. Recent Hazor remains show a quadruple entryway gate, guard towers, and a double wall. Further archaeological evidence shows that Megiddo and Gezer were built with the same kind of gates, towers, and walls. Hand-burnished pottery shards have also been found in Gezer and Hazor, dating to the twelfth century BC, when Solomon ruled.

God made you—beautiful and feminine. Bask in the amazement of all that God has created. Enjoy it. Wonder. Let it lead you to a place of mystery, and greater faith.

Becoming more aware of the many wonders around you can enhance your outlook, and your relationship with God. What are a few you can begin with? Where does your amazement send you?

_____

_____

_____

Some mysteries are hard to get past. What have you found to be beyond your wisdom? How can you turn that into a prayer of delightful acceptance?

_____

_____

_____

_____

Mysteries remind you that God is big, which can fill you with peace. Where in your life right now do you need a big God, who is wonderfully powerful and creative?

_____

_____

_____

_____

Stir in a Little Thanks

Do not be anxious about anything, but in everything, by prayer and petition, with thanksgiving, present your requests to God. And the peace of God, which transcends all understanding, will guard your hearts and your minds in Christ Jesus. Finally, brothers, whatever is true, whatever is noble, whatever is right, whatever is pure, whatever is lovely, whatever is admirable—if anything is excellent or praiseworthy—think about such things.

Philippians 4:6–8 NIV

The Big Picture

Paul wrote many letters to the churches he established on his missionary journeys, but for Philippi he had a particular fondness.

His beloved Philippi was a Roman colony and the location of Paul's first European church. Lydia, a talented business woman from Thyatira, lived there. He and his missionary companion, Silas, met her and others at a prayer meeting by a riverbank outside the city gates. Already a worshipper of God, she eagerly accepted the message of salvation through Jesus. She opened her home as a meeting place for others in Philippi who had become Christians.

Paul had other memories of his time in Philippi, like the possessed slave girl who ran along behind him and Silas as they went about the city. When they prayed for her, and she was healed, they stirred up the wrath of her keepers. They were both flogged and thrown into Philippi's old Roman jail. That was the night of the earthquake.

Paul and Silas had been praying and singing hymns when it happened. The prison walls shook so violently that the cell doors rattled open. The

take a CLOSER look for women

chains slackened. They could have walked out. Instead, Paul and Silas stayed and calmed the distressed guard. The miracle had shaken the guard as much as the earthquake. He became convinced that what the men had been teaching about Jesus was true. He tended to their injuries and took them to his home. His whole family believed Paul's message also.

Philippi—what a visit that had been for Paul. What an incredible start to the church there.

As Paul wrote to the Philippians from Rome, he must have contemplated these events. He prayed for the Philippians often, even considered them partners in his ministry to share the message about Jesus. He missed them. And they had so graciously sent a gift to him while he was in Rome. Their love and support filled him with joy.

It was easy for Paul to compose a letter expressing that joy. He included words of encouragement and guidance. He told them to treat each other with servant hearts, to be like Jesus, the greatest servant of all. And when they struggled, could they remember to keep pressing forward in their goal? Yes, he needed to address particular disputes. And before he closed, he reminded them to always pray for their concerns instead of becoming anxious.

He had much to write to Philippi, beloved Philippi.

Continue steadfastly in prayer, being
watchful in it with thanksgiving.

Colossians 4:2 ESV

When Paul wrote to the Philippians, he encouraged them to share all their worries and concerns with God. That was the easy part. He also mentioned that those prayers were to be said *with* thankfulness. Wise Paul knew that this often-missing ingredient would change their perspective, and result in a supernatural God-given peace.

He knew because he had experienced it. When Paul composed his letter to the Philippian Christians, he was under house arrest and in chains. His journeys, beatings, and imprisonments had also taken a toll on him. Still, Paul was able to write a letter filled with thankfulness—in the midst of circumstances worthy of great anxiety.

So he told the Philippians to replace the time spent in worry with time spent in earnest worship and prayer for their concerns. He said that these were to be poured out with *eucharistia,* expressions of gratitude to God for all his mercies.

Consider how thankfulness lightens your perspective. For Paul, it kept his focus on what was good, true, just, pure, and lovely, instead of on the chains of his circumstances. As a result, he felt a God-given tranquillity and quietness of soul; that *phroureo* kept watch over his mind and heart. What better way to face the anxious circumstances of life.

> For me prayer is an aspiration of the heart, it is a simple glance directed to heaven, it is a cry of gratitude and love in the midst of trial as well as joy.
>
> Saint Therese of Lisieux

As a woman you fill many roles, but sometimes the tasks involved tumble on top of one another. Just when you feel as if you're gaining a little control, something else happens. Anxiety is heaped upon anxiety. Sometimes it is so intense, your health is affected.

God delights in being your burden-bearer. Tell him of each worry and welcome his help. But then take a moment, even in the midst of the craziness, to look for those things you can be thankful for.

Gratitude is a language. In this case it's a worship language. Paul wasn't suggesting that you love the cause of your anxiety; he was saying that within it you can find God's peace *when* you stop to worship him. The thankfulness part focuses on the kindnesses you have received from him. Those have often been obscured by the tension and turmoil of your worry. Bring them to the forefront again. What is good and lovely, pure and just? What is worthy of your notice and your worship? Consider those. When you do, the awful things may not suddenly go away, but they will seem smaller, more manageable.

Let us come into his presence with thanksgiving; let us make a joyful noise to him with songs of praise!

Psalm 95:2 ESV

In *Notes from the Bible,* Albert Barnes encouraged his readers to discover those things they could be thankful for in the midst of their anxieties:

"We can always find something to be thankful for, no matter what may be the burden of our wants, or the special subject of our petitions. When we pray for the supply of our wants, we may be thankful for that kind providence which has hitherto befriended us. . . . The greatest sufferer that lives in this world of redeeming love, and who has the offer of heaven before him, has cause of gratitude."

Linda Dillow, in her book *Calm My Anxious Heart,* pointed to the difficulty of offering your requests to God with thanksgiving:

"Not only are we to pray specifically, we are to pray with thanksgiving. This is beyond difficult! . . . Psalm 116:17 helps me to understand what it means to pray with thanksgiving: 'I will sacrifice a thank offering to you and call on the name of the LORD' (NIV). I like this reminder because giving thanks when a black tunnel has enveloped my world is definitely sacrificial!"

Zooming **In**

Today, the term *eucharista* is used for the Christian observance of the Eucharist, or communion—when wine, or grape juice, and bread, representing the blood and body of Jesus, are received. The term applies the idea of gratitude for God's mercies to this traditional remembrance of Jesus' sacrifice on the cross.

Most of Paul's letters were dictated to an *amanuensis,* a servant or artistic assistant, who wrote "by hand." His amanuensis, Tertius, was more of a companion and secretary, rather than a literal servant. He added his own note to Paul's letter to the Romans, which indicates that Paul trusted him.

Gratitude is a beautiful way to bring your worries down to size, but it isn't easy to do. It means deliberately focusing in a different direction, rather than on the overwhelming cause of your anxiety.

Through the
Eyes of
Your Heart

In the midst of stress, it's hard to remember the "lovely" things God has done, and be thankful. How about recalling them now, and then write them down so you can read them later during a difficult time?

_____

_____

_____

It helps to identify the core of your worry, so you can pray more specifically about it. Then you can wrap that in another specific: what about this is good and pure and worthy of thanking God for?

_____

_____

_____

How do you enjoy being creative? In what ways can you use this in your personal expressions of gratitude and worship? Write down a few ideas and try them.

_____

_____

_____

_____

Alone with God

> Jacob was left alone, and a man wrestled with him till daybreak. When the man saw that he could not overpower him, he touched the socket of Jacob's hip so that his hip was wrenched as he wrestled with the man. Then the man said, "Let me go, for it is daybreak." But Jacob replied, "I will not let you go unless you bless me."
>
> Genesis 32:24–26 NIV

The Big Picture

For a good part of his life, Jacob was more cunning than wise. His name meant "supplanter." One night, by a quiet river, God changed that.

Jacob was on his way home after a lengthy, and not so happy, stay in Haran with his in-laws. His father-in-law had tricked him into marrying one daughter, and then working an additional seven years for the one he originally wanted. After many more deals and deceptions, God directed Jacob to return to his homeland. He left secretly with his two wives, twelve sons, many servants, and a hefty quantity of livestock. That's hard to do quietly. After a confrontation, and with an angry father-in-law-in-pursuit, God sent ministering angels to assure Jacob that he would have safety during the rest of his journey home.

If only Jacob had remembered that promise. He was about to enter his twin brother Esau's territory. He was understandably terrified. Jacob had tricked him out of his inheritance and their father's blessing. Esau had wanted to kill Jacob, and so he fled. Now Jacob was about to face his brother again.

take a CLOSER look for women

Jacob sent messengers ahead to make peace, but they returned with news that Esau was coming with four hundred men. Jacob scrambled to divide his servants and flocks into two camps, hoping that some would survive the onslaught. He then cried out to God for deliverance. God reminded Jacob of his promise to make his offspring as numerous as the sand of the sea. That meant he would make it through. To be sure, Jacob sent gifts ahead to soften Esau's heart toward him. Then he settled in to worry some more.

That night, Jacob took his family and possessions across the river Jabbok, and returned to the other side alone. Or so he thought. Suddenly, he was wrestling with a man who had incredible strength. They struggled all night. Just before daybreak, the man touched, and dislocated, Jacob's hip joint. The battle came to an end, but Jacob clung to the powerful stranger. He realized that it was not a man he had wrestled with face-to-face, but God. And he wasn't destroyed? What mercy. Still, to Jacob it looked like a great opportunity to ask for a blessing. Amazingly, he received one. God renamed him Israel—from "Supplanter" to "He who struggles with God."

Jacob was known for his persistence from birth, an attribute that continually led him to trust in his own wit and strength. At the river Jabbok he discovered God's.

God sends no one away empty except those who are full of themselves.

Dwight L. Moody

Even with God's continued assurance, Jacob became terrified of the perceived threats ahead and took matters into his own hands. A closer look reveals that Jacob believed in God, but he didn't trust him yet. God was willing to take extra and intimate measures to bring him into that trust.

This time God came to Jacob in the form of a man, not to comfort and console, but to "wrestle." This is the only place the Hebrew word *abaq* is used in the Old Testament. It's a unique word for a rare, and intimate, encounter with God. It was physical, mental, and spiritual. *Abaq* also means "to get dusty." It wasn't a wimpy tussle, and it wasn't a dream.

At first Jacob didn't realize he was wrestling with God. He seemed to hold his own for a time, but God always held the power. God demonstrated it when, toward daybreak, he ended the struggle with only a touch, and threw Jacob's hip permanently out of joint. While still entangled, Jacob discovered his opponent's identity.

God had purposely drawn Jacob away from the crowds to be alone with him. In that one-on-one, extremely physical encounter, God showed Jacob that his presence and his strength can be trusted.

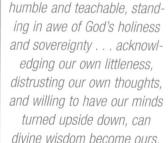

> *Not until we have become humble and teachable, standing in awe of God's holiness and sovereignty . . . acknowledging our own littleness, distrusting our own thoughts, and willing to have our minds turned upside down, can divine wisdom become ours.*
>
> J. I. Packer

It's human nature to be independent. Jacob sure had that down. All his life he trusted in his wit to pull him out of a difficult spot. It worked frequently enough to be convincing—at least until he was about to face Esau. That had him panicked.

Maybe you've found yourself wavering somewhere between "I can do it myself," and "Okay, God I will trust you." Sometimes it takes practice to learn how to trust the assurance God continually gives. Sometimes it takes more. As with Jacob, God may design a unique one-on-one encounter just for you.

It could be a moment in the garden, your hands in the soil, tugging at a weed. Maybe it's an interaction with a child who is resisting your love—suddenly you feel as if you're looking at yourself. Take notice of whatever gentle lesson God is giving you, and stop struggling against him. Instead, lean into him in trust.

Thankfully, what you've got coming at you is not only a powerful God, but one who loves you and will do what it takes to convince you that he's worth trusting. That makes the wrestling worth it.

Humble yourselves, therefore, under the mighty hand of God so that at the proper time he may exalt you.

1 Peter 5:6 ESV

E. M. Bounds believed that a one-on-one wrestling with God is essential to your prayer life. In *Power Through Prayer* he said:

"Our short prayers owe their point and efficiency to the long ones that have preceded them. The short prevailing prayer cannot be prayed by one who has not prevailed with God in a mightier struggle of long continuance. Jacob's victory of faith could not have been gained without that all-night wrestling."

In *Notes on the Pentateuch,* C. H. Mackintosh considered Jacob's wrestling a turning point, an example of how people can gain a correct view of themselves:

"No matter what we may think about ourselves, nor yet what man may think about us, the great question is, what does God think about us? And the answer to this question can only be heard when we are 'left alone.' Away from the world; away from self; away from all the thoughts, reasonings, imaginations, and emotions of mere nature, and 'alone' with God—thus, and thus alone, can we get a correct judgment about ourselves."

Zooming **In**

The Jabbok, where Jacob wrestled with God, is one of the main tributaries into the Jordan River. Today it still originates out of a vigorous spring near the modern city of Ammon. It is now known as Zerka, or "blue river," because of the color of the water. Many consider it to be one of the most picturesque rivers in Palestine today.

Jacob and his brother, Esau, are the first twins mentioned in the Bible. Jacob's ancestors became the Israelites; Esau's, the Edomites. Archaeological evidence indicates that the kingdom of Edom was established in the thirteenth century BC. Tribal chiefs ruled first, and then kings. Eight Edomite kings reigned before Israel named its first king.

Do you ever feel as if you're moving through your days on your own? Find a favorite cozy spot to think about this. How might you invite God to join you?

_____

_____

_____

God is definitely worth trusting. During your times alone with him, in what ways does he assure you that this is so? How is he doing that right now?

_____

_____

_____

It takes practice to remember God's promises, and to act on them in a moment of panic. What are your natural reactions? How can God help you through the next time?

_____

_____

_____

An Invading Awe

When Simon Peter realized what had happened, he fell to his knees before Jesus and said, "Oh, Lord, please leave me—I'm too much of a sinner to be around you." For he was awestruck by the size of their catch, as were the others with him.

Luke 5:8–9 NLT

The Big Picture

A woman dresses and slips on her shoes. She expects it to be just another day—like yesterday and the day before—but maybe it won't be. Some days seem to begin quite ordinarily, and then fill with events that change your life. That's what happened to Simon Peter.

The morning sun had begun to peek over the eastern hills and glimmer on the quiet Galilean sea. Birds screeched overhead. Waters lapped at the shore, and a common fisherman named Simon bent to clean his nets after a long, unsuccessful night of fishing. As any fisherman would be, he was tired, ready to head home. Then Jesus showed up, and the unexpected happened.

At the opening of this story, Jesus had begun his three years of public ministry. He was about to gather men to work alongside him. His arrival at the Sea of Galilee followed forty days of fasting, facing Satan's temptations in the wilderness, and several days of teaching and healing others. As you can imagine, Jesus' teaching and miracles stirred up the growing crowd. Many followed him through the night and into the morning.

When Jesus approached the fishermen who were washing their nets, he asked Simon to take his boat out from the shore so Jesus could teach the people. Simon did. As he steadied the boat and listened to Jesus' words, he was unaware that the coming moments would change his life.

Jesus finished teaching, turned to Simon, and said, "Let's go fishing." You can imagine what Simon thought. He had worked all night. The Greek word *kopiao* used for *work* means "to labor with exhausting difficulty." And indeed, the men had, as they cast their weighted nets into the sea, and then pulled them back in empty, time after time. Yet at Jesus' request, Simon willingly took the boat out again. What happened next completely surprised him.

The nets overflowed with fish and almost broke. Quickly, Simon and his friends signaled for the men in the other boat to help. The load of fish almost sank both vessels. Those fishermen had never hauled in a catch like that.

Amazement seized Simon and his fishing buddies, James and John. You see it in Simon's response: "Oh, Lord, please leave me—I'm too much of a sinner to be around you." Jesus calmed them, and then turned the catching of fish into an invitation to join him in catching people for the kingdom of God. Those three men were the first of twelve to leave everything to follow him.

Life is not measured by the number of breaths we take, but by the moments that take our breath away.

Author Unknown

Though he had yet to understand that Jesus was God, Simon sensed there was more to this good teacher and performer of miracles. Look closely at Simon's reaction to the miracle. Overwhelmed, he fell to his knees. He begged Jesus to go away. A life-changing awe overtook Simon, like a sudden storm upon a sea.

Jesus knew the fishing trip was more than a call to fish for men. He wanted to capture Simon's heart, so he used something Simon would understand: fish. Nets bursting with the flipping and flopping creatures would make sense to Simon—except that he'd never seen so many. The bursting nets amazed Simon more than if Jesus had used any other illustration.

Those nets also exposed Simon's heart more than anything else could have. You sense it in his anguished words. The contrast of their two lives must have been as clear to Simon as the difference between the empty nets of his first fishing attempt, and the overabundance of the second. The latter caused an astonishment that invaded his whole being. The Greek word used here is *periecho*, which means "to surround or encompass, to seize and take possession of." His astonishment was more than simple surprise. It was an amazement that possessed, and took over.

> *Before He furnishes the abundant supply, we must first be made conscious of our emptiness. Before he gives strength, we must be made to feel our weakness.*
>
> Arthur Pink

That was a remarkable moment for Simon Peter. It could happen to you, too. But if you knew it would expose your heart, as it did Simon's, would you run the other way? For Simon, the miracle, and its accompanying revelation, came unexpectedly. He thought he was just fishing. Then it happened, and he was stuck in a boat. He couldn't run. All he could do was fall to his knees and beg Jesus to go away.

But Jesus didn't go away, and he won't go away from you either. Just as Jesus stayed when he saw Simon's heart exposed and imperfect, he will stay with you. He will allow the awe to wash over the moment and invade your life. It is a gift, an amazing, agonizing gift—one you can long for over and over again.

Perhaps you've had a life-changing event like Simon's, or you soon will. Know that Jesus doesn't want you to be so overwhelmed by the contrast of your life with his that you ask him to leave. You are his beloved. He wants to capture your heart.

His mercy flows in wave after wave on those who are in awe before him.

Luke 1:50 MSG

It might be that the life-changing event Simon Peter experienced was necessary to prepare him for the service he would do for others. Cecil Murphey, in *The Relentless God*, said:

"This appears to be the first major step toward taming and molding Peter for his position of leadership. From other accounts, we know he's perceptive, quick-thinking, bold, and a natural leader. Is it possible that he might also be intolerant and unable to accept others who are less able? Could it be that the Holy first strikes him within and asks, 'See this?' Once Peter recognizes himself as vile and sinful, he's ready for divine use. He's ready to fish for people and bring them to God."

It may well be that's the message for all of us. Until the divine light flashes within, we don't hear or grasp the messages that God persistently sends us. Then one day, seemingly in some ordinary context, the Holy breaks into our lives. We hear the truth for the first time.

Zooming **In**

Tilapia, one of the most popular farm-raised fish in the world today, is likely one kind of fish that Peter caught in the Sea of Galilee. For that reason, since biblical times, it has also been known as Saint Peter's fish. You can still order it by that name in some restaurants today.

The Sea of Galilee is a small sea with several other names, including the Sea of Tiberias or the Lake of Gennesaret. Known for its beauty and the fertile soil near its shores, ancient rabbis said of it, "Jehovah hath created seven seas, but the Sea of Gennesaret is His delight."

*Awe that brings you humbly to your knees helps you
to see the depth of God. What an opportunity to catch
a view of his character, and let it change your life.*

God used the uniqueness of who Simon Peter was to bring about a specific, life-changing moment. How has God used who you are as a woman, and an individual, to uniquely reveal himself? How has that changed you?

_____

_____

_____

God is amazingly pure and perfect. When you spend time with him, do you sometimes feel exposed and imperfect? How can this draw you closer to him?

_____

_____

_____

_____

The miracle in Simon's life took him into a new adventure with God. Is he doing that with you? Where is he taking you?

_____

_____

_____

_____

New Places

> The LORD said to Abram, "Go forth from your country, and from your relatives and from your father's house, to the land which I will show you; and I will make you a great nation, and I will bless you, and make your name great; and so you shall be a blessing."
>
> Genesis 12:1–2 NASB

The Big Picture

The world Abram was born into was a very different one than existed when the Flood receded and his great (plus, plus) granddad Noah stepped off the boat. The ground had long since dried. Noah's descendants were numerous and spreading across the region. Thoughts and devotions once again turned away from God to made-up gods. This must have saddened the ancient Noah greatly. He lived 350 years past the Flood, and watched his own family forget God. But he was alive when Abram was born. Perhaps he saw a ray of hope, but he had to look past Abram's father, Terah, to find it.

Abram's family lived in Ur, a thriving city near what is now known as the Persian Gulf. The people there, including some of Abram's ancestors, worshipped a moon god. When Abram grew up and married Sarai, Terah moved all of them, along with Abram's nephew Lot, away from Ur. They traveled far north to a place called Haran, another city filled with cults and gods. In both

take a CLOSER look for women

cities, Abram's father Terah himself may have been involved in some cultic worship. It was Terah's choice to stay many years in Haran, instead of moving on to a more desirable city. It was where he grew old and died.

God did not forget Abram. Just after Terah died, God directed Abram to leave his country, his people, and his father's household, and go forward to another land called Canaan. It would be hundreds of miles from Haran or Ur. God promised that he would bless Abram in this new place. His name would be great. He would live in a land of endless potential, and his family would become so numerous, they would become a nation.

The Bible doesn't record any doubt or argument on Abram's part. It simply says, "So Abram went as the Lord had told him." He was seventy-five years old when he left Haran, with his wife and nephew, to travel to a place with so many unknowns. What would it be like? Would they be safe? Would they find a home? They would have to trust God.

As they packed their belongings, perhaps they thought about Noah. He was gone by then, and did not know about God's special call on his descendant, but Abram would carry on his legacy of faithfulness.

Wherever you are, be all there. Live to the hilt every situation you believe to be the will of God.

Jim Elliot

At first glance, Abram's response to God's call seems so simple and willing. Get up and go. No problem, especially when you attach all those promises and blessings. But was it that easy for Abram? Perhaps not.

It's just a general list, but look at what Abram was asked to leave: the country of his birth, his relatives, and his father's house—everything he had known and grown comfortable with. Both Ur and Haran were part of Mesopotamia, and shared common culture. Add that familiarity to those he loved and the home he'd known. Abram had roots there.

Now he was to travel to an entirely new place. He might have heard a little about Canaan from passing travelers, but did he really know what he was getting into? The culture would certainly be different. Family-wise, he left only with Sarai and his nephew Lot. And as wonderful as God's promise sounded, there was that one part about making him a great nation. Everyone knew Sarai was barren.

Though it isn't recorded, Abram must have struggled with all this. No matter how willing he was to honor God's request, it was a difficult move. Yet he trusted.

> *God is God. Because He is God, He is worthy of my trust and obedience. I will find rest nowhere but in His holy will, a will that is unspeakably beyond my largest notions of what He is up to.*
>
> Elisabeth Elliot

Change can be difficult, no matter what form it comes in. What is easy is getting really comfortable with where you are, and what you've had. Unfortunately, things don't usually stay that way forever. At some point you will probably find yourself facing a move of some kind that you weren't ready for.

It might be a job change, or a move to a new neighborhood or city. It might involve others in your family, or going alone. If you've enjoyed creating a place that feels cozy and reflects who you are, the change can be especially difficult.

Emotions stir and stomachs churn when it comes to big changes. Sometimes hurts are involved or maybe unfinished business. As you look ahead to the move, questions fill your mind: What's ahead? Will I like it? Will I be okay?

You can be sure that as you pack those special dishes, photos, or mementos, you're taking someone important with you—God. Even if you can't see the full picture yet, you can trust him. God, who had a plan in place for Abram and Sarai, has one in place for you.

"I know the plans I have for you," says the LORD. *"They are plans for good and not for disaster, to give you a future and a hope."*

Jeremiah 29:11 NLT

How Others
See It

F. B. Hole, in his article "'Come On' and 'Get Out,'" reflected on what the people of Ur might have thought about Abram's move to Canaan:

"When Abram turned his back on the splendid Ur of his day, his action must have appeared to be the height of folly to the men of his generation. 'Why,' they would say, 'you are throwing away all your chances. You leave civilization and plunge into the unknown. No monument will ever be erected in Ur to perpetuate your distinguished name to future generations!'"

J. N. Darby, in an article from the 1800s, wrote about the example that Abram gave to all believers:

"The earth was not only now corrupt and violent—it had departed from God. It had not liked to retain God in its knowledge, and served other gods. God, in sovereign election, calls Abram to follow him apart from the world; and separation from the world for the enjoyment of promise by faith becomes the divine principle of blessing. Abraham is the father of all them that believe."

Zooming **In**

Life spans in biblical times were pretty amazing. Noah lived for 950 years. Environmental factors and food may have contributed, but some scientists give credit to the chromosome. These scientists say Noah was genetically programmed to live longer. Life spans began to reduce, however. Abraham died at the age of 175, Sarah at 127.

Haran, along with most Akkadian or Sumerian cities, had its favorite patron god. It shared worship of the moon god Nanna, with its sister city, Ur. When Akkadian and Sumerian cities united under the Assyrian conqueror, Sargon, all their gods were adopted into one elaborate mythology. The number of gods reached over three thousand as new gods were added.

God may call you to "go forth," out of your comfort zone, to a new place or situation. Know that as you are following his direction, he will help you in the adjustments.

Through the
Eyes of
Your Heart

God has created you to uniquely express your femininity wherever you go. Can you believe that if God moves you to someplace new, he will help you feel at home again?

_____

_____

_____

Moves can be filled with all kinds of emotions. Do yours include hurts and unfinished business? What can you do to move on with more peace?

_____

_____

_____

_____

So much is ahead for you, but when you can't see the full picture, questions and concerns fill your mind. How can you see change as part of God's plans, moving you to a better place?

_____

_____

_____

Just One Touch

A woman who had hemorrhaged for twelve years slipped in from behind and lightly touched his robe. She was thinking to herself, "If I can just put a finger on his robe, I'll get well." Jesus turned—caught her at it. Then he reassured her: "Courage, daughter. You took a risk of faith, and now you're well."

Matthew 9:20–21 MSG

The Big Picture

After twelve years of doctors, and countless unsuccessful remedies, the sick woman in this story was likely poor and close to death. By Jewish law, she was deemed unclean. She was not to come in contact with anyone, or they, too, would be considered unclean. As she made her way through the streets, did she wrap a faded veil around her face and wonder if she should have come?

She had heard much about this Jesus. Was he a different kind of physician? She couldn't go on much longer, weakening each day as she was. But the stories about all the miracles and healings gave hope. Jesus had been preaching in the areas around Galilee. Every day more and more came to hear him speak, and to receive his miracles of healing. By all the excitement in the streets, she knew she must be getting closer. She slowly made her way, one frail step at a time.

Somewhere in the crowd, a ruler of the synagogue at Capernaum spoke to Jesus. His daughter was dying, and he wanted to know if Jesus would make her well. Jesus rose to follow the grieving father.

As he came down the road, the woman saw him. It might have been the only opportunity she'd have. She wouldn't disturb him. She only needed to get a little closer. The crowds likely jostled her about as she wondered if she would get her chance.

But then he did come closer. All she had to do was reach out and touch the hem of his garment, that's all. If only . . . if only . . . there! One moment she felt the fringe brush the tips of her fingers and the next . . . she felt her strength return. Then she heard him say, "Who touched me?" As he looked around, she drew in her breath. What would he do? Should she run?

His eyes landed on her. Trembling, she went forward and knelt before him to confess that she had touched his garments. She timidly explained why, and then waited. He must have seen her fear, for he comforted her: "Take courage, daughter. Your risk of faith has brought your healing."

She was healed. It was just a moment, a stop along the road, but in one touch, twelve years of suffering came to an end.

It matters little what form of prayer we adopt or how many words we use. What matters is the faith which lays hold on God, knowing that He knows our needs before we even ask Him.

Dietrich Bonhoeffer

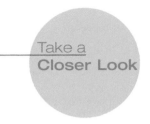

A whisper of faith is all it takes. Look closely. See that the actions of the woman in this story were as quiet as she could make them, but they were packed with a simple and genuine faith. That faith would accomplish far more than physical healing.

The woman who had suffered horribly for twelve years, slowly, but resolutely, made her way to Jesus. "I shall be whole," she said to herself just before she touched the fringe on Jesus' robe. *Whole* in Greek is *sozo*. It refers to being "saved from death," but is also used to mean "saved from eternal death." Which one she meant is not known, but it is clear Jesus responded to her silent request, and saved her both physically and eternally.

Without her saying a word, Jesus understood all the struggles and faith behind the touch she risked. The Greek word used for *touch* is *haptomai*, and means "to attach oneself to" or "to bind." It was more than a simple touch, just as her belief to be healed was more than a simple wish. Jesus knew and called her "daughter." She was healed and bound to him forever.

> *Our fear cancels our faith, but if we choose to take the risk of faith, we soon learn that it was our fears that were the real risk.*
>
> Gary V. Carter

The woman who touched Jesus' robe felt crippled by her medical issue, and how others viewed her. She longed for health and wholeness. Years of trying to attain that left her poor, and growing weaker every day.

Apply It
to Your Life

It may not be an illness that has crippled you. It could be other circumstances you've struggled against to try to live a fuller life. But perhaps you've found that every attempt to make it better leaves you more discouraged. It's hard to fan that last flicker of hope and keep it burning.

The woman tried many doctors and avenues of healing before she heard about Jesus. When she touched Jesus' robe, it wasn't the amount of faith she had, but the genuineness of the little faith she had left.

Maybe you feel that your faith has a few thin spots. It doesn't matter as long as what you have is directed toward Jesus. He is always working, healing hearts and bodies, but he's never too busy to stop for you. In your hope for something better for yourself, be courageous. Take the risk to reach out to him with what faith you have right now.

Everyone who has been born of God overcomes the world. And this is the victory that has overcome the world—our faith.

1 John 5:4 ESV

Some wonder if the hemorrhaging woman believed that Jesus' garment had supernatural powers. In his *Commentary on Matthew 9*, J. B. Coffman said:

"It is plain from this that Jesus rejected whatever of superstition there may have been in the woman's act. A suspicion that some element of superstition might have motivated her comes from the fact that she touched a particular part of his garment supposed to be especially holy. . . . His plain words made it clear to the woman that he, of his own will, had healed her."

In his commentary, Matthew Henry took a tender view of the woman, and focused on her faith:

"But what weakness of understanding there was in it, Christ was pleased to overlook, and to accept the sincerity and strength of her faith. . . . She believed she should be healed if she did but touch the very hem of his garment, the very extremity of it. . . . There is virtue in everything that belongs to Christ."

Zooming **In**

In the tradition of Jewish dress, Jesus probably wore an outer garment in the shape of a square or oblong. It would be thrown over the shoulders. The "hem of the garment" was a fringe, or *tsitsith*, which the authorities commanded Jews to wear to distinguish them from other nationalities.

The physicians in Jesus' time were not greatly esteemed. You never knew if you had one that could help, or one that only pretended to cure illnesses. Either way, most administered horrible-tasting medicines. Some used herbs and folk remedies, including such ingredients as alum, saffron, Persian onions, and cumin. These might be stirred into wine before being given to the patient.

take a CLOSER look for women

Your faith is not measured in its exuberance as much as in its genuineness. God sees the quietest expressions of faith.

When you're discouraged, it's hard to muster the energy to change your situation. What are a few simple ways you can use what strength you have to purposefully move toward God?

_____

_____

_____

Jesus isn't physically with you, but he is available for you to turn to, just as the woman did. In reaching out to touch him, what are you hoping for? Can you tell him about it?

_____

_____

_____

Does your faith feel a little thin right now? Risking what faith you have at this moment can only make it stronger. As he tells you, "Courage, daughter," what do you discover about his love for you?

_____

_____

_____

_____

Ready to Catch You

*When he noticed the strong wind, he became fright-
ened, and beginning to sink, he cried out, "Lord, save
me!" Jesus immediately reached out his hand and
caught him, saying to him, "You of little faith, why
did you doubt?"*

Matthew 14:30–31 NRSV

The
Big Picture

The wind and waves can be excellent tools for learning a little about yourself—and a lot about Jesus. With
these ingredients, Peter was in for another lesson.

Jesus and the disciples had an exhausting day.
They had gone to Bethsaida to rest after days of ministry around Galilee, but thousands had followed
them. Jesus taught and performed healings and miracles, then felt it was
time to move on. He sent the disciples ahead in their boat, while he went to
the mountain to pray. He would meet them later, on the other side of the Sea
of Galilee.

It was nighttime when the disciples launched out to cross the little sea. The
disciples who had been fishermen were accustomed to the sea in all kinds of
conditions. They had no reason to anticipate trouble. But just as they
reached the middle of the sea, a storm hit. The winds lashed against them,
and the waves grew more violent. The disciples were soon in danger.

Through the dark and the crashing waves, they saw a figure moving

take a CLOSER look for women

toward them. It was so unusual, it was frightening. But from the sea came a familiar voice. "Be comforted and don't be afraid. It's me." Incredibly, it was Jesus walking on the crests of the waves.

Peter wanted to be with him, and called out to him, "Lord, if it's you, ask me to come to you on the water." Jesus said, "Come."

Peter didn't jump in and swim; he stepped out onto the sea and walked. Pure devotion led him toward Jesus. The wind, growing more blustery than before, whirled around him. He paused and saw its strength. Perhaps at that moment, he remembered the impossibility of what he was doing, and the danger of the storm. He began to sink. "Lord, save me!" he called as he slid into the dark waters.

Instantly Jesus stretched out his hand and grabbed Peter. "Oh, Peter, your faith is small. Why did you doubt?"

Together they walked back across the waves to the boat, and the wind died down. The disciples were astounded, and they worshipped Jesus. He really was the Son of God. You can imagine Peter huddled in the safety of that boat, quietly wrestling with the miracle of that event and his wavering faith in the presence of one so mighty and able.

Though a particular course of undertaking of yours failed, you are still a beautiful creation of God.

Stanley C. Baldwin

When Peter walked on the water and began to sink, he learned something new about the condition of his faith. He also learned something about Jesus: he is powerfully near and personal.

The sudden storm hit when the twelve men were almost halfway across the sea. Jesus knew they were in trouble. He could have calmed the waves from the shore. Instead, he personally showed up to save them. He came to the disciples in the boat, and then responded directly to Peter's courage and devotion. From the sea, he looked at Peter and told him to come.

Jesus already knew about Peter's boldness, so the request to come out onto the stormy waves wasn't a surprise. When Peter's courage wavered and he began to sink, Jesus was there immediately, stretching out his hand. The Greek word used for *hand* is *cheir*. Applied to God, it symbolizes his power that is always present, always protecting.

Jesus, the one who could command the waves to be still and could command Peter into the boat, chose to take the personal route by stretching out his hand to save. He is the Son of God, worthy of worship, but he is also near and personal.

> *We trust not because a god exists, but because this God exists.*
>
> C. S. Lewis

Do you have a situation where you need the kind of trust that kept Peter on top of the waves? Maybe it involves a relationship you've hoped to nurture, a dream you've wanted to pursue, or a ministry you've worked hard to launch. Now it feels impossible to take that next step. Where are your eyes focusing?

Apply It
to Your Life

Are you seeing the winds of every detail that threaten to sink you? Doubts arise that you'll ever see your hopes to a satisfying end, and fears pull you down. Instead of moving ahead, you want to climb back to safety.

But what is safety? What is right? Where are those who once supported me?

Jesus is out there with you, right in the midst of the unruly winds and rising waves. You can trust that he is more powerful than anything that threatens to pull you under. He cares about the uniqueness of where you are, and where you're heading.

"You can do it, my daughter," he tells you as he reaches his hand toward you. "I will stay near," he says as he walks alongside. "Together we'll walk on the crest of the waves."

I'm not saying that I have this all together, that I have it made. But I am well on my way, reaching out for Christ, who has so wondrously reached out for me.

Philippians 3:12 MSG

Andrew Murray, in *The Deeper Christian Life,* noted that when Peter forgot the presence of Christ, Jesus restored it:

"Yes, Christ took him by the hand and helped him, and I don't know whether they walked hand in hand those forty or fifty yards back to the boat, or whether Christ allowed Peter to walk beside Him; but this I know: they were very near to each other, and it was the nearness of his Lord that strengthened him."

In one of his sermons, turn-of-the-century preacher Alexander MacLaren spoke of Jesus' invitation for all to come nearer:

"There are none of us so close to Christ but that we can't come nearer, and the secret of our daily Christian life is all wrapped up in that one word of invitation from Jesus, 'Come.' That nearness is what we are to make daily efforts after, and that nearness is one capable of indefinite increase. We know not how close to His heart we can lay our aching heads."

Zooming **In**

The Jews didn't have watches, so how did they tell time? The Hebrew day was divided by descriptions of temperature: "the time the sun is hot," mid-morning; "the heat of the day," noon; and "the cool of the day," evening. Nighttime was divided by a rotation of watchmen, so the divi- sions were called "watches." The Jews had three, but Roman influence added one more. They landed at approximately 6:00 p.m., 9:00 p.m., midnight, and 3:00 a.m. When Jesus went out on the water toward the disciples, it was during the fourth watch, or around 3:30 a.m.

Jesus is powerfully near and personal. When circumstances seem to rise up against you, he may not calm them, but he can meet you in the midst of them.

In those next difficult steps to reach your goals, Jesus' hand is ready to catch you if your courage begins to falter. What situations are the most difficult to trust him with?

_____

_____

_____

Peter's unreserved devotion and trust in Jesus kept him above the waves. How can you strengthen your love for him so you can keep him as your focus?

_____

_____

_____

_____

Jesus is not far away commanding all the details. What details most concern you? How can you bring him into those on a daily basis?

_____

_____

_____

_____

Let Me Be an Answer

"If she gives me a drink and offers to get some water for my camels, I'll know she is the one you have chosen." Even before I had finished praying, Rebekah came by with a water jar on her shoulder. When she had filled the jar, I asked her for a drink. She quickly lowered the jar from her shoulder and said, "Have a drink. Then I'll get water for your camels."

Genesis 24:44–46 CEV

The Big Picture

Eliezer rode steadily toward the city gates of Haran. He was on an important mission. He was being sent to find a wife for Isaac, his master Abraham's son. She couldn't be from Canaan, only from Haran. Eliezer promised he'd find the right one, but he would need God's help.

His aging master trusted him, but this wasn't going to be easy. He would be freed of his oath if a suitable wife refused to come, but he hoped for success. Thankfully, Haran had possibilities. It was still home to some of Abraham's people.

He drew his camels up near the well to rest. It was evening. The women would soon come to draw water. He hoped that among these he would find Isaac's bride. Before any arrived, he knelt and prayed fervently, and specifically, that in response to his request for water to quench his thirst, the right one would say, "Please drink, and let me water your camels."

Before he completed his lengthy prayer, a beautiful maiden came through the gate toward the well, balancing her water jar on her shoulder. Eliezer ran

take a CLOSER look for women

to meet her and asked for a drink. She immediately served him, and then offered to draw water for the camels as well.

Was this the one? Eliezer watched her in silence. As she finished watering the camels, he lavished her with gifts of gold—a nose ring and two bracelets. Then he asked who she was. Rebekah from the house of Nahor. Nahor was Abraham's brother! Eliezer fell down and praised God for his faithfulness in answering his prayer.

Rebekah offered her family's home and barns to Eliezer and his camels. That evening, as they were about to eat, he told them how God had blessed his master. He had become great in the country of Canaan. The servant then explained his mission, and how Rebekah had specifically answered his prayer. He hoped they would allow her to go with him. They consented, and Eliezar offered gifts to Rebekah and her family. In the morning he requested that she go with him right away, so they called her into the room.

"Rebekah, will you go with Eliezer to be Isaac's wife?"

"I will go," Rebekah replied with confidence.

Soon after, Eliezer left with Rebekah and her nurse. God, in his love and care, answered Eliezer's prayer in the smallest detail.

When we allow God's love to fill our lives and to spill onto others, the life that God has prescribed for us happens naturally.

Kay Marshall Strom

Rebekah watched as Eliezer bent his head to worship God for his answer to prayer, but it wasn't until later that she discovered she was the answer. A closer look reveals that Rebekah responded to God in a way that made her available to move right into the middle of his plans.

As is true for most who are answers to prayers, at first Rebekah was not aware of Eliezer's specific appeal to God. Her humble response to his request for water showed her willingness to be kind, and to serve others. In fact, she *quickly* served him. It did not matter who he might be. Further, she showed Eliezer hospitality in offering her family's home for lodging. Rebekah showed all this kindness before she knew his mission, or his relationship to her relative Abraham.

Eventually, in her home, Eliezer explained the entire story, including the prayer. Rebekah learned that she had responded exactly as he had prayed. Then she was given the chance to say no to Eliezer's request to go with him right away. She said, "I will go."

One action after another, and then three simple words, all showed the kind of heart ready to be an answer to prayer.

> *All the service that weighs an ounce in the sight of God is that which is prompted by love.*
>
> Billy Sunday

You, too, can be an answer to someone's prayer.

Rebekah's response to Abraham's servant had to have sprung from a habit of loving and serving others. She didn't hesitate. Her lifestyle, and her caring heart, put her in a good place to naturally be an answer to prayer.

Apply It to Your Life

You can begin by emulating God's character and his ways toward you. Look at how he's available to you: He is patient, personal, and always there. He is also kind and loving. It doesn't matter who you are, he cares deeply about what is important to you. Make these your ways of responding to others, and you're sure to be an answer to someone's prayer.

But it takes far more than good character. At the time Rebekah said, "I will go," she had learned a little more about what God was asking of her. With her words, she responded to God as much as, if not more than, she did to Eliezer.

A lifestyle that emulates God's character, plus an understanding of what God asks of you, and a readiness to respond to him, all work together to put you in the best place to be an answer to others' prayers—even those you may not know about.

Do nothing from selfishness or empty conceit, but with humility of mind regard one another as more important than yourselves; do not merely look out for your own personal interests, but also for the interests of others.

Philippians 2:3–4 NASB

You can be an answer to the prayers you pray for others. In *Handle with Prayer,* author and pastor Charles Stanley said:

"When praying for others, we must be willing to be part of the answer if necessary. If we aren't willing to be used to answer our own prayers, we aren't cooperating with God. As a result, He won't cooperate with us; He won't answer our prayers. Why? Because these are prayers of isolation and separation. We are saying, 'God I don't want to get mixed up in anyone's problems. *You* take care of that.'"

Oswald Chambers wrote about being an answer to a prayer uttered centuries ago:

"I want to share with you a growing conviction with me, and that is that as we obey the leadings of the Spirit of God, we enable God to answer the prayers of other people. I mean that our lives, my life, is the answer to someone's prayer, prayed perhaps centuries ago."

Zooming **In**

Eliezer, Abraham's servant, was trusted to manage the household affairs. He was with Abraham long before his master had children, and was called a "son of his house." Abraham even appointed him as an heir. He had been in service for fifty or sixty years at the time Abraham sent a "senior servant" to find a wife for Isaac.

Abraham lived in Bethel on the edge of the Negev desert, a desolate area that covers more than half of Israel. Today you can take a camel safari through the Negev and see where Abraham journeyed four thousand years ago. A caravan might stop to view one of Abraham's ancient wells. Travelers would rest overnight in a rustic Bedouin-style camp.

It's a privilege to be an answer to prayer. Each day brings new opportunities to be an active participant in God's unfolding plans.

Through the
Eyes of
Your Heart

Rebekah saw needs and served. What strengths has God given you to help others? How might they be used as an answer to someone's prayer?

_____

_____

_____

_____

When your loving actions become habits, you are readily available to be a part of God's plans. Do you have a friend who has a need? How might you show love toward her today?

_____

_____

_____

Each person can be a part of what God is doing in the lives of others. What does this show you about those who are kind to you? What does it show you about God?

_____

_____

_____

The Scarlet Signal

The men said to her, "This oath you made us swear will not be binding on us unless, when we enter the land, you have tied this scarlet cord in the window through which you let us down, and unless you have brought your father and mother, your brothers and all your family into your house."

Joshua 2:17–18 NIV

The Big Picture

After many nomadic days in the desert, it was time for the Israelites to enter the land of Canaan—to take the land God had given them. Joshua, their warrior leader, told the people to prepare to cross the river Jordan. In the meantime, he sent two spies to investigate what they were up against, particularly in Jericho.

The two men forded the river and traveled the seven miles to the city. They stayed at a home within the outer walls, owned by a woman named Rahab. The woman was a prostitute, and her house was also an inn. Word spread to the king that the two spies were there. He sent his men to find them.

It must have been a tense moment for all. The spies knew they were discovered, but not in time to leave. Rahab hid them among sheaves of flax she had laid out to dry on the roof. As the king's men barged in and inquired about the spies, she told them they had been there, but she didn't know who they were. She said they left at dark before the gate was closed, and encouraged the king's men to go quickly to catch up with them.

take a CLOSER look for women

Rahab hid the spies because she had heard the stories of how God had helped the Israelites out of Egypt and through the Red Sea. He had given them victory over many kings. She and the people of Jericho were afraid. "Your God," she said, "rules the heavens and the earth." She believed in this God.

After the spies came down from the roof, Rahab appealed to them for help. She had been kind to them. Would they swear to save her, and her family, when the Israelites came to destroy Jericho? They promised. She was to tie a scarlet cord in the window, and gather her family into her house. The spies instructed her that none were to leave when Israel attacked. They then climbed down the scarlet rope to the ground outside the city, and returned to their camp.

Soon the Israelite army arrived, and marched around Jericho. On the seventh day they miraculously took the city with shouts and trumpet blasts. In an unusual story of God's power and mercy, all of Jericho crumbled except for the portion of the city wall where the scarlet cord hung in Rahab's window. She and her family were saved.

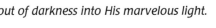

You are a chosen race, a royal priesthood, a holy nation, a people for His possession, so that you may proclaim the praises of the One who called you out of darkness into His marvelous light.

1 Peter 2:9 HCSB

To Rahab the scarlet cord meant the salvation of her family. As she hung it in her window, she had to trust that the Israelites would see it, and honor what it represented. She had to trust God. That trust was tested.

When the spies left, Rahab's waiting time filled with a mixture of trepidation and trust. What would happen when the Israelites attacked the city? Rahab had heard of the strength of their powerful God. Now he was her God, too. Would he protect her?

The Israelites came and marched for days. Which of those would come for her? They hadn't said. On the seventh day, the walls began to crumble. Had they forgotten? She wasn't to leave, no matter what. Would she and her family die in the rubble?

Rahab's thoughts, and possible fears, are not recorded, but the story's account shows that she did just as she was told. That simple symbol, the scarlet cord, remained in her window throughout the siege. She and her family obeyed. They stayed in her home in the wall. She had nowhere else to go, but to trust in the promise of a scarlet cord.

> *I've been driven many times to my knees by the overwhelming conviction that I had nowhere else to go.*
>
> Abraham Lincoln

In Jericho, Rahab lived a heartbreaking existence. Who knows what circumstances caused her to, at one time, choose the lifestyle she did. Even if she was no longer a harlot when the spies came, she likely felt utterly worthless. Her home was within the city wall where she eked out a living serving guests. But when no one else seemed to care, God stepped in and rescued her, not only from Jericho, but also from her hopeless life.

Apply It
to Your Life

Though your life may not feel as empty as Rahab's, you might feel no one cares about the choices you have made and where they've taken you. The painful patterns that seem to endlessly repeat themselves have trapped you in your own Jericho walls.

Do you know that God keeps pursuing you? In his great love for you, he works tirelessly to turn your face toward his, so you can see he cares for you. Your scarlet cord is Jesus; the cross, his final rescue. That's what you can hang in the window of your life. God sees it, and will bring you out of your own Jericho walls.

They stripped off Jesus' clothes and put a scarlet robe on him.

Matthew 27:28 CEV

The "scarlet line" stretches from Rahab's window to yours. William Easton, an author from the late 1800s and early 1900s, would have agreed:

"And what does Rahab's window say to us as Christians? Surely it reminds us in a forceful way that God's Son is coming from Heaven to deliver us from this doomed world. He has already saved our souls; the scarlet line hangs out of our windows; we are sheltered by the precious blood of Christ, indwelt by the Holy Spirit and are now waiting for the Lord Himself to come and take us home."

Another turn-of-the-century author, H. A. Maxwell Whyte, also noted the scarlet thread through biblical history. In *The Power of the Blood,* he said:

"The Israelites sprinkled blood in Egypt and it brought deliverance! Rahab used the blood-line token and it brought deliverance! The High Priests of the Old Testament sprinkled blood and it brought forgiveness! Jesus sprinkled His own Blood and purchased salvation for all mankind!"

Zooming **In**

Scarlet was a rich crimson color used for royal, or expensive, garments. It was also used in the Jewish tabernacle of the Old Testament. The dye was made from the eggs of a beetle often found on the holm oak trees of Palestine. In Arabic, these are called *kirmiz*, from which the English word *crimson* is derived.

Though it has had three sites, Jericho is considered one of the oldest cities in the world. It is also called the city of the palms, which reflects its tropical climate. In ancient times, the date palm and balsam trees did well there, and balsam medicine became a lucrative business. Today Jericho is a popular winter tourist place.

The scarlet cord is a beautiful picture of rescue and relationship. In each rescue, God saved an individual or nation from peril, and then brought the people to a place where they could know him.

Through the
Eyes of
Your Heart

When Rahab was rescued, she left her old life behind in the rubble of Jericho. What about your life would you like to leave behind? What hopeful future does God show you?

_____

_____

_____

God's scarlet rope for you is his Son, Jesus. Blowing free in the frame of your window, it means relationship with him. Do you trust him? Do you doubt? Tell him.

_____

_____

_____

Has your scarlet rope been in your window for a long time? Does it seem tattered and forgotten? How might you freshen up your view of God and your relationship with him?

_____

_____

_____

Watching for You

"I will arise and go to my father, and I will say to him, 'Father, I have sinned against heaven and before you. I am no longer worthy to be called your son. Treat me as one of your hired servants.'" And he arose and came to his father. But while he was still a long way off, his father saw him and felt compassion, and ran and embraced him and kissed him.

Luke 15:18–20 ESV

The **Big Picture**

Jesus is often known as "the Word." It's no surprise, then, that he had a way with words.

The Pharisees had long since begun to despise Jesus, and the claims he made. They watched him closely for violations of their Jewish laws, and easily found cause for criticism. Jesus often responded with questions that made them think, and he told parables.

When they grumbled about Jesus' spending time with what they considered the filth of society—the "publicans and sinners"—he told three parables. Each highlighted the value of what was lost and the importance of finding, and bringing it back. One was the story of the prodigal son.

This is a story about a man, with an extensive inheritance, and his two sons. The younger son came to him to request his share, and the father willingly divided his property. A few days passed, and the younger son decided to take all of his inheritance and explore his options elsewhere. He traveled far away from his family, and all that he had been taught. It wasn't long before he wasted everything he had through his reckless choices.

Shortly after, a famine hit. He had nothing to survive on, so he hired himself out to one of the local men who had him feed his pigs. His provisions were so scanty that he craved the pods he fed to the pigs.

Understandably, he began to think about home. He thought, *Even my father's hired servants have more than they can eat, and here I am dying of hunger.* Right then he decided to go home and ask forgiveness. Maybe he could work as one of his father's hired men, and at least have a warm bed and a little food to stave off his hunger.

As he was on the road nearing his house, his father saw him and ran to meet him. He celebrated his son's return, but his older son became jealous. The father longed for him to understand the joy he had in his lost son returning home.

Jesus told this story to the Pharisees and scribes, and in the presence of the "publicans and sinners." He hoped all would understand the longing of God to, like the father, bring home his lost children. For some of the listeners, it meant seeing their "brother" with more compassion. For others, it was an invitation to return home.

*It is quite true to say, "I can't live a holy life,"
but you can decide to let Jesus make you holy.*

Oswald Chambers

**Take a
Closer Look**

This story is known for demonstrating God's forgiveness of his wayward children. Zoom in on one particular part, and you see that the father began to welcome his son home before the son had a chance to recite his speech, and ask for forgiveness—even "while he was still a long way off."

The younger son's return to the father's home came in steps. He lost everything, tried to survive anyway, realized his mistakes, understood his need of forgiveness, and then began his journey home. The entire time, the father hoped with all his heart he would one day enjoy a reunion with his son—so much so, that he always watched the road.

One day his long wait was rewarded. The story says that even as the son was coming from a distance, the father saw him, and felt compassion. He didn't wait for him to arrive at his gate, but ran to meet him. He then showered him with expressions of his love, and his joy.

You can imagine what a son would feel, seeing his father watching for him, then running toward him on the road, arms stretched out, eager to embrace him. That's the love of God the Father.

> *God's mercy was not increased when Jesus came to earth, it was illustrated.*
>
> Eugenia Price

Jesus' stories are for all people of all times. This one tells of God's patient love and ready forgiveness, even *as* his child is returning to him.

You likely can remember a time when, as a little girl, you made a foolish decision that you regretted when you realized it would disappoint someone. Whether or not you did it defiantly, you knew you deserved discipline. And you probably recall how awful you felt—the guilt, the fear of going and confessing, and asking for forgiveness.

Those uncomfortable feelings can be tender gifts. They are reminders that you've traveled into places that can only hurt you. But don't let them hold you in fear away from God and those who want to offer forgiveness. God, the Father, eagerly watches for each child's homecoming. Even when there are hurts that need working through, "home" is a better place to be.

Whether it's you or someone you know who needs to return to God's loving arms, be assured he sees you no matter how far away you feel, and he's waiting to welcome you back.

The Lord is not slow in doing what he promised—the way some people understand slowness. But God is being patient with you. He does not want anyone to be lost, but he wants all people to change their hearts and lives.

2 Peter 3:9 NCV

The father saw his son while he was still far down the road. Sandra Wilson, in *Into Abba's Arms,* compared this to being "brought near by the blood of Christ" (Ephesians 2:13 NASB):

"I'm beginning to *experience* being 'brought near' as I draw closer to Jesus in regular times of solitude. In effect, I keep on being brought near. I continue to come back to Jesus. I think maybe that's the secret to living in increasing intimacy with Christ: keep responding to his call to come home.

"God has been calling us home to his arms, where we belong, since the Garden. His call fills the far countries and rattles the pigpens. If we dare to believe, we'll hear it. Now, depending on how far the country and how filthy the pigpen when we flee our Father's will, we may have to limp, stagger, or crawl on hands and knees. It doesn't matter how we get there. We need to keep coming back to Jesus."

Zooming **In**

Parabole is Greek for *parable.* It comes from *para,* meaning "near or beside," and *ballo,* meaning "to cast." So, a parable casts one idea beside another for the purpose of illustrating a religious, moral, or philosophical insight. It is different from a fable in that it keeps to the natural order, and speaks about spiritual matters.

The "husks," fed to the swine in this parable, were really bean pods from the kharub, or carob tree. The pods were six to ten inches long, and had a gel-like substance inside. Today the carob tree grows primarily in Africa and other arid regions, and is considered fodder for cattle and antelope.

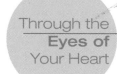

Some life choices take you away from God, whether for a moment or much longer. Dear daughter, when you start heading toward him again, you can be certain he has been watching for your return.

Returning to God is a process. The goal is to stop destructive behavior, and again live within the boundaries of his love and plans for you. Are you at home with God, or returning somewhere along the road?

_____

_____

_____

Sometimes a return to God involves asking him, or others, to forgive you for hurtful choices. The forgiveness is there, but you won't know that until you ask. Is anything keeping you from asking?

_____

_____

_____

In coming back to God the Father, you have nothing to fear. Imagine a loving Father eagerly waiting to embrace his daughter. Describe what you see.

_____

_____

_____

_____

A Purpose Beyond You

When the child grew older, she brought him to Pharaoh's daughter, and he became her son. She named him Moses, "Because," she said, "I drew him out of the water." Years later, after Moses had grown up, he went out to his own people and observed their forced labor.

Exodus 2:10–11 HCSB

The
Big Picture

One day, a little baby was born, and someone already wanted to kill him. God had another plan.

Jacob and his family had fled to Egypt during a famine, while his son Joseph worked for a kind pharaoh. He allowed them to live in the fertile land of Goshen, and their numbers grew. Eventually Joseph and the pharaoh died. By that time, the Hebrew people had grown so numerous, they could be a nation.

The new ruler felt threatened by these Hebrew people. To wear them down, he gave them difficult jobs. When that didn't work, he made them his slaves. He also asked their midwives to sabotage the births of baby boys. None of this worked. The Hebrew people continued to grow in numbers. In rage, the pharaoh told his people to throw all Hebrew baby boys into the Nile River, but let the daughters live. He hoped this growing nation of Hebrews would disappear.

In a little house in the middle of this chaos, a Hebrew couple gave birth to a son. She nursed and hid him for three months. The growing baby, wriggling and crying, became more difficult to hide. The mother made a basket out of bulrushes, and waterproofed it with bitumen and pitch. She put him among the reeds of the river where his older sister could watch from a distance.

After a while, Pharaoh's daughter came to bathe at the river, and discovered the baby boy. She knew he was Hebrew, but she felt sorry for him. The baby's sister stepped forward and offered to find a Hebrew woman to nurse him—of course that would be her mother. The baby lived at home until he grew a little older. The mother then took him to the pharaoh's daughter, who gave him the Hebrew name Moses, meaning "to draw out."

All this time, the pharaoh continued to abuse the Hebrew people. When Moses became a young man, he realized what was happening. One day he saw an Egyptian beating a man. Angered, Moses killed the Egyptian and hid him in the sand. The pharaoh found out and wanted to kill him, so he fled to a place called Midian.

Moses, even as a young man brought up in the pharaoh's household, did not forget his roots. He didn't want to see his people treated so poorly. Though he escaped to Midian for forty years, he didn't forget the oppression of his people.

Everything, absolutely everything, above and below, visible and invisible, rank after rank after rank of angels— everything got started in him and finds its purpose in him.

Colossians 1:16 MSG

The pharaoh's daughter gave Moses his name, but she didn't realize how prophetic it was. *Moses* also means "one who draws out" or "deliverer." God, the ultimate deliverer of all, planned for Moses to be rescued as a baby, so that one day he would deliver all his people. Moses had a purpose before he understood it, and beyond what he'd ever know.

Pharaoh's order to kill the baby boys was horrific. Only Moses is known to have survived. These kinds of situations bring up the question "Where was God?" He was there. Throughout history man has sought to destroy, and God responds by saving. Egypt was no different. Many were killed, but God's plans for his people would not be thwarted. A river that was death for many became life for the nation as a little baby was found alive in a basket, floating among the reeds.

When Moses fled Egypt as a young man, it seemed to be the end of the usefulness of his name—but it wasn't. God still planned to deliver all of his people from the evil pharaoh. He brought Moses back to "draw them out" of Egypt to safety. God saved one Hebrew baby, who grew up to save them all.

> For the Christian, there are, strictly speaking, no chances. A secret Master of Ceremonies has been at work.
>
> C. S. Lewis

Like Moses' name, many names have special meaning: Hannah means "Grace"; Abigail, "My father is joy"; and Sarah, "Princess."

Apply It
to Your Life

Your name may or may not have anything to do with how God might use you. Still, like Moses, your life has amazing purpose beyond what you can imagine right now. When you consider this, it can change your perspective and the way you live out each day.

But, you say, what you do seems so insignificant. Don't believe that for a moment. Your life is like a tiny seed that has grown into a beautiful annual flower. It produces more seeds for more flowers. Put in the right environment for which it was designed, a flower multiplies its purpose. So can your life.

You are significant to God. You always have been. Who you are, and what you do, matters. Today matters. Each choice you make to do something on behalf of God's purposes, he will multiply far beyond what you'll ever be able to imagine.

Let this truth change how you might live this day differently. See the potential. Strive for your best. Somewhere, tucked into what seems routine, is the beautiful unfolding of the purpose of you.

The good soil represents the hearts of those who truly accept God's message and produce a huge harvest—thirty, sixty, or even a hundred times as much as had been planted.

Matthew 13:23 NLT

Grasping the importance of your purpose will drive your life in new directions. Rick Warren, in *The Purpose Driven Life,* said:

> "The purpose of your life is far greater than your own personal fulfillment, your peace of mind, or even your happiness. It's far greater than your family, your career, or even your wildest dreams and ambitions. If you want to know why you were placed on this planet, you must begin with God. You were born *by* his purpose and for his purpose."

With a fully devoted heart, you can live out God's purposes beyond your wildest imaginings. Charles E. Cowman, in *Streams in the Dessert,* said:

> "The world is waiting yet to see what God can do through a consecrated soul. Not the world alone, but God Himself is waiting for one who will be more fully devoted to Him than any who have ever lived; who will be willing to be nothing that Christ may be all; who will grasp God's own purposes; and taking His humility and His faith, His love and His power, will, without hindering, continue to let God do exploits."

Zooming **In**

The basket, or *tebah,* that Moses' mother made for him, was also called an "ark," because it was much like a little boat. She fashioned it from reed stalks of the bulrushes that grew along the banks of the Nile. The woody part of these reeds was often used by the Egyptians to build light, sturdy boats to use on the river. Moses' miniature ark was smeared with tar-like pitch to make it waterproof and buoyant. It had a cover to keep him safe, and was set among the reeds of the Nile so it wouldn't float away.

God continued to work through the nation Moses saved. His Son, Jesus, was born to a Hebrew woman. Do you see the long, unfolding history of God's purposes? It continues, and you're a part of it.

This very day matters. You matter. You really do. Where do you struggle with believing that?

_____

_____

_____

_____

Moses' life had purpose even before he knew it. Yours does, too. God's purpose for you has already been set into motion. Look closely at your life as a woman of God's design. What do you see so far?

_____

_____

_____

Even if your part seems small, what you do is significant in God's scheme of things. Can you catch the greater, eternal vision of what God is doing? How can you participate?

_____

_____

_____

Wings of Refuge

Boaz answered her, "Everything you have done for your mother-in-law since your husband's death has been fully reported to me: [how] you left your father and mother, and the land of your birth, and [how] you came to a people you didn't previously know. May the LORD reward you for what you have done, and may you receive a full reward from the LORD God of Israel, under whose wings you have come for refuge."

Ruth 2:11–12 HCSB

The Big Picture

Ruth looked tenderly toward her mother-in-law. "Naomi, it's harvesttime," she reminded her. "Should I go find a field where they will let me gather the left-behind grain?"

"Oh, yes, daughter. That would be good."

Naomi had suffered much loss after she and her family left Bethlehem during a famine. The years of refuge in Moab had been heartbreaking. Not long after they arrived in the foreign country, Naomi's husband died. Later her sons married, but then they also died.

When Naomi decided to return to Bethlehem, she encouraged her Moabite daughter-in-laws, Ruth and Orpah, to return to their families. Ruth chose to honor the Hebrew custom to serve her deceased husband's family. She loved Naomi and had grown to love God. "I will go with you," she told her. "Your people are now my family. Your God is my God."

Dear Naomi. Her name meant "pleasantness," but in her sadness and loss, she told her friends to call her Mara, meaning "bitter." She said, "I went out full, and came back empty."

take a CLOSER look for women

Hebrew law made provision for the poor to glean the grain dropped by the harvest reapers. Perhaps Ruth could soften Naomi's suffering by gathering food for them. She didn't realize she would choose a field belonging to Boaz, a relative of Naomi's husband.

Ruth watched Boaz while he walked among his workers and spoke to them. He treated them well. He glanced toward her as he talked to one, then turned and came toward her.

"My daughter, glean only in my fields," he gently told her. "Gather where other young women are working."

Was he concerned for her safety? True, the fields could be dangerous for a foreigner, and a woman working alone. His kindness touched her.

He went on. "I've told my young men to treat you with respect. When you are thirsty, drink only from the vessels of water they have drawn."

In gratitude, she dropped to the ground before him. "Why are you being so kind? After all, I am a foreigner."

"I've heard how well you have cared for Naomi," Boaz told her. "You left your family, and country, to come here to this new place. Surely God, under whose wings you have sought refuge, will reward you for all you've done." What encouragement that brought to Ruth. She had found a safe haven in Bethlehem, and in Boaz's fields, as she experienced God's protection and care of her and Naomi.

There is not in the world a kind of life more sweet and delightful than that of a continual conversation with God.

Brother Lawrence

A young bird nestles into the warmth and safety of her mother's feathers. Poignant and hopeful—isn't it? It's a picture of God's refuge. But look closer. This refuge is not only for your moments of need; it's an ongoing relationship.

Ruth's choice to seek refuge in God was a lifetime commitment. She chose to leave Moab, an immoral and arrogant nation that worshipped different gods. She committed to a new life in Bethlehem. Boaz heard she had set her devotion toward taking care of Naomi, and serving God, even from the time of her husband's death.

Ruth's devotion led her to a place of refuge under God's wings. "Refuge," or *chasah,* means to "confide in, have hope in, put trust in." These were the actions of Ruth's heart. She sought refuge, and found a new spiritual dwelling place with God—an ongoing relationship with him.

God would "reward" Ruth. Two Hebrew words are used. *Shalam* means "complete" or "prosper." *Maskoreth* means "wages." He would complete and prosper her diligent service and trust. The "wages" of Ruth's faith was God's continual grace and protection; she was no longer a foreigner, but one of God's own.

> *God will never, never, never let us down if we have faith and put our trust in Him. He will always look after us. So we must cleave to Jesus. Our whole life must simply be woven into Jesus.*
>
> Mother Teresa

It's encouraging to watch a mother bird hide her young under her wings.

When you need his protection or rescue, God gladly ushers you into a place of spiritual safety. But as you've seen in Ruth's story, you don't need to wait until you feel overwhelmed, or vulnerable, before you find refuge under God's wings. That refuge is a right-now relationship between you and God. And it's ongoing.

"Under his wings" is a place for you to get better acquainted with the one who offers his continual grace and protection. It's a place to deepen your trust of him, begin to confide in him, and talk to him about anything and everything. It's a place to feel at home.

When you were hurt or scared as a little girl, you ran to a place that felt safe and familiar, to a person whom you knew would understand and love you. Make yourself at home under God's wings of refuge. Get to know him well. When difficulties arise and you need him, you'll be turning to someone who has become familiar.

Trust in him at all times, O people; pour out your hearts to him, for God is our refuge.

Psalm 62:8 NIV

The image of God's wings gives a beautiful picture. In his sermon "Ruth's Reward," Don Fortner offered several possibilities for this image:

"The metaphor used by Boaz to describe Ruth's faith refers either to the wings of the cherubim overshadowing the mercy-seat; or to the wings of a mother hen. In either case, it speaks of a place of great strength, complete safety, personal care, and great comfort. Christ is that hiding place for sinners. In him, we take refuge under the wings of the Almighty."

In an *Every Day Light* devotion called "Under His Wings," Selwyn Hughes encouraged the downhearted to draw into the shelter of God's wings:

"Some of you have stood for God despite great criticism from your families and friends. He has seen all your tears, all your heartache, and all your sacrifices. And He promises you a perfect reward one day. Draw close to Him now and nestle beneath the shelter of His great wings. Look up and see how easily they cover you. Under His wings there is no further need for tears—just trust!"

Zooming **In**

Even though its name means "house of food" or "bread," the town of Bethlehem in Judah experienced a severe famine. The most common cause for famines in the ancient Near East was lack of rainfall. It wasn't unusual for families, or even a whole country, to leave in order to find food.

Allowing the poor to glean grain left behind by the reapers was a custom that had its roots in the old Levitical law. If harvesters forgot a bundle of grain, they were to leave it for a foreigner, a widow, or the fatherless. Those who did not follow this law could be punished. Some Syrian field owners still encourage gleaning today.

In choosing God as her refuge, Ruth discovered a relationship that flowed into each day, and into every area of her life. That's the kind of refuge God offers you.

Through the
Eyes of
Your Heart

God spreads his welcoming wings and invites you to come to him now, not just when you feel you need his refuge. How will you "step under his wings" and get to know him Father-to-daughter?

_____

_____

_____

As an expression of her choice to follow God, Ruth moved away from Moab to Bethlehem. What in your life would you move away from as you move into a deeper trust in God?

_____

_____

_____

In a right-now, ongoing relationship with God, he is available for you to confide in him any time. What longings or heartaches would you share with him right now?

_____

_____

_____

The Danger of Being Hungry

After fasting forty days and forty nights, he was hungry. The tempter came to him and said, "If you are the Son of God, tell these stones to become bread." Jesus answered, "It is written: 'Man does not live on bread alone, but on every word that comes from the mouth of God.'"

Matthew 4:2–4 NIV

The Big Picture

With John's strong arm cradling his back, Jesus broke through the surface of the flowing Jordan and stood. Water streamed off his face and shoulders, and he watched God's Spirit come down from the heavens in the form of dove. It rested on him, and all present heard God's voice: "This is my Son whom I love, my greatest delight."

Jesus' cousin John had just baptized him, God introduced him, and then within days, if not moments, God's Spirit led him into a nearby desert. In that lonely place inhabited only by wild animals, Jesus would face *diabolos*—the "devil," the "false accuser." You have heard him called Satan.

This evil one was a *peirazo*, a tempter, and the best there was at tempting. His goal? As always—destroy God and anything he loved. This time he would attack Jesus. He saw it as a perfect opportunity. In that barrenness, Jesus was isolated. No friends to warn him. No supplies or food to keep him strong.

For forty days and nights, Jesus fasted. He faced the vulnerabilities of desert exposure and hunger. The accuser nagged and harassed, but waited until the right time—the forty-first day—to use his most deceptive tricks.

The tempter sneered. "Ah, you must be starving. If you really are the Son of God, you could make these desert stones into bread. Why don't you?"

Jesus sensed the sham. "God has said, 'Man can't exist only on bread.' My food is God's truths." Jesus trusted in the goodness of his Father, and the timing of his provision.

The tempter persisted. He supernaturally whisked Jesus to Jerusalem, and placed him on the highest point of the Jews' holy temple. "So you think you're God's Son? Throw yourself off this pinnacle. Hasn't God said that he will tell his angels to protect you? Prove it."

Jesus again applied God's words. "God has said not to test him."

Satan tried once more. This time he transported him to a high mountain with a view of many glorious kingdoms. "You can be ruler over all of this. Just worship me."

"Go away from me, Satan," Jesus replied. "In God's laws it says that I am only to serve and worship him."

"Go away," was a command from Jesus, God in the flesh. Satan had to obey. After the tempter left, angels came and tended to the Son of God. He had defeated *diabolos*, the *peirazo*, not with weapons, but with God's own words.

This same God who takes care of me will supply all your needs from his glorious riches, which have been given to us in Christ Jesus.

Philippians 4:19 NLT

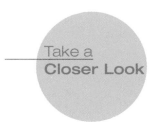

Chocolate cravings are one thing, but there are hungers that take so thorough a hold, they leave you exposed. Look at the point at which Satan chose to use his most powerful temptations. It was at the end of Jesus' forty-day fast—when he was hungry. In fact, it was when he was nearly dying. That's what the peirazo does—he looks for those opportunities of greatest vulnerability.

The Son of God, draped in the limitations of humanity, was physically vulnerable. He had eaten nothing for an extended length of time, and his body was shutting down. Satan knew Jesus was God's beloved Son. He knew that Jesus was sent to challenge his dominion. He wanted Jesus destroyed. This time he thought he could win. In his eyes, Jesus seemed defenseless in the desert—alone and starving.

Satan could not win then, or ever. In the flesh, Jesus felt the agony of human need. Through his hunger he experienced the deepest, and darkest, temptations Satan could devise. But Jesus was more than a man. He was the Son of God, sent to overcome; he would not give in.

He conquered any hunger he might have for food, power, or glory. He did it for God the Father. He did it for you.

Oh, that we would turn eye and heart from everything else and fix them upon this God who hears prayer until the magnificence of His promises and His power and His purpose of love overwhelms us.

Andrew Murray

Satan's methods have not changed. His fingers of temptation sense opportunity in your moments of weakness. What better occasion than when you are starving to be cherished and understood, to be free from the drudgery of routine, to feel wanted for all of who you are as a person and as a woman. Being hungry can be dangerous.

Apply It
to Your Life

When you have reached the limits of your hunger, and find yourself drifting into the arms of compromise, remember Jesus in his wilderness. God had you in mind when he sent him to face intense conditions and temptations. Jesus was tempted in his human body in ways beyond what any would experience. So he understands the longings in your wilderness. He understands the ways you are tempted to satisfy them.

Jesus also understands what works to overcome even the most enticing temptations. He used words from the Bible, words he knew by heart. Meditate on the Psalms. Pull out phrases you can use for your prayers. Read what Jesus, and others, said when they faced difficult situations. Write out the Scriptures that speak directly to your hunger. Commit them to memory. Use God's words as Jesus did. Overcome.

You can trust God, who will not permit you to be tempted more than you can stand. But when you are tempted, he will also give you a way to escape so that you will be able to stand it.

1 Corinthians 10:13 NCV

God made provision for spiritual hunger. Martin Luther spoke of this in "The Temptation of Christ":

"In spiritual matters this temptation is powerful when one has to do with the nourishment not of the body but of the soul. Here God has held before us the person and way by which the soul can be forever nourished in the richest manner possible without any want, namely Christ, our Saviour. But this way, this treasure, this provision, no one desires. Everybody seeks another way, other provisions to help their souls."

In consideration of Jesus' fast, Frederick Louis Godet discussed the condition of hunger. In the *Pulpit Commentary—The New Testament*, he said:

"In certain morbid conditions, which involve a more or less entire abstinence from food, a period of six weeks generally brings about a crisis, after which the demand for nourishment is renewed with extreme urgency. The exhausted body becomes a prey to a deathly sinking. Such, doubtless, was the condition of Jesus; he felt himself dying. It was the moment the tempter had waited for to make his decisive assault."

Zooming **In**

Though unsuitable for city development, the Judean wilderness has been a place of refuge for those on the run from their enemies . . . or a place of retreat. During the Byzantine period, sixth century AD, this wilderness became home to monks who sought seclusion. A network of trails connected sixty-five monasteries, with a distance of only two or three miles between the retreat centers.

Jesus fasted for forty days. The most common emulation of that today is the Christian observance of Lent, which begins forty days before the celebration of Easter. Individuals might participate in a limited fast, giving up certain foods, like meat or sweets, in order to focus on prayer and God's grace given through Jesus.

Hunger of any kind puts you in a state of vulnerability. Jesus, who resisted the tempter when he was most vulnerable, can help you through your hungry moments.

What do you hunger for most as an individual? As a woman? How do these needs make you vulnerable? Make you compromise?

_____

_____

_____

_____

God knows the depths of your hunger. What are ways you can be still with him, and trust him with your longings?

_____

_____

_____

_____

Saturating your mind with God's words, and remembering his hopes for you, will help you resist making harmful choices. What do you know right now that will encourage you?

_____

_____

_____

The Now of Grace

Our high priest is able to understand our weaknesses. When he lived on earth, he was tempted in every way that we are, but he did not sin. Let us, then, feel very sure that we can come before God's throne where there is grace. There we can receive mercy and grace to help us when we need it.

Hebrews 4:15–16 NCV

The Big Picture

The Bible book of Hebrews is a letter about an ongoing love story—a story that began with the creation of man and woman. The letter begins, "Long ago and for many centuries, God spoke to your Hebrew ancestors through the prophets, but now he speaks through his Son Jesus."

In that long-ago time, God created a beautiful world and breathed life into his first created humans. But Satan, like a villain seeking to corrupt and destroy, intruded into their perfect love relationship. This evil one succeeded in his plan to mar the heart of God's beloved. He introduced mistrust, deception, and selfishness, which sent the human heart far away from God.

For thousands of years God sought to restore his relationship with each man and woman. He'd do anything to regain their love. Anything—even die. He had a plan. For a while, through the Hebrew nation, he showed what sacrifice was needed. He provided special laws, asked for smaller—but important—sacrifices, put into office men called high priests, and created a way for their wrongs to be forgiven—a way for them to begin to know him again. These worked for a time, but the sacrifices had to be done over and over again. A greater sacrifice was still needed.

One day God stepped into his beloveds' world as Jesus, and put on human skin and clothing. People talked to him and touched him, but often didn't recognize him. He worked hard while in the world and loved each one. Again he confronted Satan. This time the villain attempted to thwart any plan God had to reclaim the hearts of his beloved. It seemed as if the villain succeeded. The people remained blinded to God's love for them. They rejected him again—even helped kill him.

But Jesus became the Great Sacrifice who so powerfully, and painfully, ended all sacrifices. People could be freed of their past, and any hold the villain had on them. Until each one understood this, God would keep pursuing and wait.

Through its beautiful presentation of who Jesus is, the book of Hebrews was written to remind the Hebrew people, and future readers, of God's pursuit of his own. You are God's beloved, his princess. In coming to live and die for you, he also became the High Priest of all priests, who declares that no more sacrifices are needed. He is the one who understands your weakness, and offers his grace.

A teardrop on earth summons the King of heaven.

Charles Swindoll

The Lover pursued his beloved—a princess dressed in a tattered, soiled gown. When you look closely, you may recognize yourself as that princess. Jesus, the High Priest who knows all about weaknesses and grace, loves you and understands the struggles you face today.

The book of Hebrews is so named because it was a letter written to Jews who professed to be Christians. Its message is unique in its emphasis: Jesus is better than anything that has come before. In fact, he is absolutely the final, and the best, in revealing God, his love, and his mercy. And he is alive, right now, and filling his days loving you.

In ancient days, God's first high priests were the only ones allowed near God's earthly throne. They entered on behalf of the people to ask forgiveness for their wrongs. Jesus became the final High Priest. He sits next to God the Father in the heavens—his new throne where he is today. He is the final Great Sacrifice, the final High Priest. At any moment you—his princess, his beloved—can go to him for help and forgiveness, and he will understand.

God is every moment totally aware of each one of us. Totally aware in intense concentration and love.

Eugenia Price

The love story continues. You are God's beloved. He is daily pursuing a relationship with you. He is aware of every joy, sadness, struggle, and victory you face. He thinks of you, calls for you, and fights for you—even this very moment.

You need to know how important you are to him. When you read the Bible from cover to cover, look closely for the thread of his love from creation to this day. He pursues you and cherishes you. He fights for you and wins the battles. He does all of this, every day, on your behalf, as he did for those in the Bible.

He sent Jesus—Immanuel, God with us. Clothed in human flesh, he faced hunger, tiredness, loneliness, and betrayal. He was challenged and tested, belittled and misbelieved. People spat on him, tortured him, and then murdered him. And yet, he overcame it all, for you, his beloved.

Know he understands your frustrations, your mistakes, your sadness, your disappointment. He cares about each difficult moment you face, and pleads with you not to face them alone. He is available and approachable right now, as your Priest, King, Lover, and Friend.

The LORD appeared to him from far away. I have loved you with an everlasting love; therefore I have continued my faithfulness to you.

Jeremiah 31:3 ESV

Jesus, as your High Priest who understands, felt temptation more intensely than anyone ever will. John MacArthur explained why in his sermon "Our Great High Priest":

"Jesus faced a much harder battle with temptation than we do. . . . There is a degree of pain we will never experience because our bodies turn off the pain before we get to that level. The same thing is true in temptation. There is a degree of temptation we never experience because we succumb long before we get to that point. Since Jesus never sinned He experienced temptation to the utmost extreme."

Many wonder if Jesus faced every type of sin and, if not, how he understands. Kent Hughes addressed this dilemma in *Hebrews: An Anchor for the Soul*:

"Does this mean that every detailed, individual sin we face he faced? No, but it does mean that there is no category of sin, no type of sin that we face that our Lord did not successfully endure. . . . You have One in heaven who truly understands and sympathizes with you in every weakness and temptation. So draw near to him with your burdened heart as you struggle on the journey."

Zooming **In**

Those who practice Judaism today don't sacrifice animals for forgiveness of sins, but a few feel this is disobeying God. The problem is that in AD 70, the Romans destroyed their temple where these sacrifices took place. The Jews would like to rebuild the temple in the original location. The site is currently occupied by the Dome of the Rock. This gold-domed building is the third holiest place for Muslims and a shrine for their pilgrims. The people of that religion believe it is where Muhammad ascended into heaven. The Bible teaches that the Jews will someday acquire that land again, and rebuild their temple.

The book of Hebrews brings Jesus into the present. He cares about all that is happening in the world today. He cares about you.

Through the
Eyes of
Your Heart

Do you feel like a princess clothed in a tattered gown? You don't have to face your mistakes and disappointments alone. Jesus is available to you right now. What will you tell him?

_____

_____

_____

One reason Jesus went through temptation and mistreatment was so you'd know he understands yours. What pain is tucked deep within your heart?

_____

_____

_____

God invites you to his throne where you will find his compassion and grace. You go there simply through prayer. What in your life needs to experience the fresh waters of his forgiveness?

_____

_____

_____

Authentic Compassion

The Pharisees saw this and asked his disciples, "Why does your teacher eat with tax collectors and sinners?" When Jesus heard that, he said, "Healthy people don't need a doctor; those who are sick do. Learn what this means: 'I want mercy, not sacrifices.' I've come to call sinners, not people who think they have God's approval."

Matthew 9:11–13 GOD'S WORD

The
Big Picture

Jesus strode through the familiar streets of Capernaum, toward the seaside where his boat was moored. Men and women smiled and whispered about him, for he had miraculously healed their neighbor. Children ran behind him. He reached down and tousled the hair of one, and grinned at another. That's what you might picture as Jesus made his way among townspeople who had seen his kindness and his miracles.

Maybe that happened. More certain, however, is that the Pharisees and scribes—Jewish religious leaders and law experts—leaned their heads together and grumbled. With furrowed brows, and shaking heads, they condemned Jesus' actions. *Who was he to command healing? To declare anyone's sins forgiven?* They'd have to keep an eye on this one.

As Jesus neared the Sea of Galilee, he stopped at the tax booth where a man named Matthew sat ready to collect fees from those who passed. Oh, and how those pious leaders despised Matthew—what a traitor. Not only had this Jewish man thrown his allegiance to the Romans, he overcharged and became rich off others. And the Roman government allowed it. All the publicans were just like Matthew—swindlers, cheaters, the filth of the street. That was the perception of many.

But not Jesus.

"Matthew," Jesus said, "follow me."

Jesus asked a disgraceful cheater to be one of his twelve special followers? Yes, he did. Without hesitation, Matthew agreed. He immediately left his booth. He'd never again return to it, or to the reputation attached to it. In his excitement, he invited Jesus to his house for a feast. Others came, too—others just like Matthew.

You can imagine what the Pharisees and scribes thought then: *Look at that gathering of the most wicked and vile in town. Despicable.*

They asked the disciples, "Why does your Teacher eat with that lowlife?"

Jesus overheard and said, "It is not the healthy that need a doctor, but the sick." Then he challenged the leaders: "Go and learn what this means: 'I want your mercy, not your sacrifices.'" Jesus must have looked at them with sadness. They seemed so stuck in their traditions. "I've come to call those whose lives are hopeless, and full of wrong living, not those who believe that God approves how they live."

Jesus knew it wasn't how bad a life someone led that kept them from coming to God; it was more often pride. He showed the way of compassion and mercy.

I would rather feel compassion than know the meaning of it.

Saint Thomas Aquinas

"Of all people, they asked *her*." We've all thought that . . . or maybe felt others think that of us. It hurts.

Jesus couldn't have picked a more despised member of the community than Matthew to join his team. When he did, he demonstrated kindness to the extreme. Then he told the religious leaders to take time to learn what this means: "I want mercy, not sacrifices" (Matthew 9:13 GOD'S WORD).

That statement was from an Old Testament Scripture, Hosea 6:6. Used in its earlier historical context, it meant that God delighted far more in an outpouring of love for him than in ritual sacrifices. Jesus quoted Hosea within a different situation to challenge the religious leaders and law experts. What Jesus said is, "Go learn what it means to live a life of compassion toward others, instead of one focused on empty religious living."

Jesus knew the futility of living by rules—no matter how sound—in order to gain God's approval. Especially when that meant being blind to opportunities to show compassion to others. Jesus showed a different way. He saw past the bleak shadows of Matthew's life to the possibilities of a hope-filled heart. He had compassion. His challenge today would be the same: go and learn to show mercy.

> *It is possible to give without loving, but it is impossible to love without giving.*
>
> Richard Braunstein

We all want to hear someone say, "Hey, I know you struggle. I know you make mistakes every day, but that's okay—I really love you."

How refreshing that would be. All that pressure to perform would be gone. You could gather those how-to-be-perfect rules and throw them to the wind. No more trying to have the perfect hairstyle, the perfect house, or the perfect response to every note. Ahhhh. Hear the sigh come from deep inside. That's relief.

Yes, Jesus called the Pharisees, and even you, to go and learn compassion for others, but sometimes that compassion needs to begin right at home—in your own heart. If you looked inside, you might find, piled up in a corner, a stack of "wish-I-hadn'ts" as tall as six months of unwashed laundry.

The Pharisees were shocked that Jesus was willing to get close to Matthew. Oooo, ick—he's dirty. Maybe that is how you feel about yourself. Jesus forgives. His mercy and compassion for you are never ending. He's willing to get close to you—no matter what you have hiding in your heart.

Let go of the rules. Grab on to him. Go; learn compassion. Begin with yourself.

Finally, all of you should be of one mind, full of sympathy toward each other, loving one another with tender hearts and humble minds.

1 Peter 3:8 NLT

How Others
See It

Being compassionate toward others might come with a price, but it's worth it. John Piper, in his February 1986 sermon "Blessed Are the Merciful," discussed the key to being merciful:

"[Mercy] grows up like fruit in a broken heart and a meek spirit and a soul that hungers and thirsts for God to be merciful. Mercy comes from mercy. Our mercy to each other comes from God's mercy to us. The key to becoming a merciful person is to become a broken person. You get the power to show mercy from the real feeling in your heart that you owe everything you are and have to sheer divine mercy."

Jesus doesn't mind getting close to any ugliness in a person's life in order to bring his love into the picture. Joni Eareckson Tada, in *The God I Love,* said:

"Ah, this is the God I love. The Center, the Peacemaker, the Passport to adventure, the Joyride, and the Answer to all our deepest longings. The answer to all our fears, Man of Sorrows and Lord of Joy, always permitting what he hates, to accomplish something he loves."

Zooming **In**

Tax gatherers, or "publicans," like Matthew bid for their position, and the Romans awarded the contract to the highest bidder. A person who made this his occupation was an outcast, having disgraced his community and his family. He was excommunicated from the synagogue and disqualified to act as a witness in court.

The religious leaders Jesus met in Capernaum were *Pharisees,* meaning "the separated ones." They also called themselves *Chasidim,* which meant "loved of God," or "loyal to God." These were the strictest of the Jewish sects. Many Pharisees became more interested in the appearance of righteousness, than genuine piety—but not all. Some even participated in the beginnings of the Christian movement.

Jesus beautifully demonstrated compassion with Matthew. His example shows you how to love others, and how to love yourself.

Through the **Eyes of** Your Heart

Do you struggle with loving yourself, or accepting something about yourself? If Jesus were to walk up to you right now, what would he see? Would it matter that you aren't perfect?

_____

_____

_____

For a moment, close your eyes and consider the mercy God has given you— the grace. How has he been compassionate toward you?

_____

_____

_____

_____

Does a fear of rejection keep you from showing compassion to others? What other barriers, or perceptions, keep you from showing kindness to others?

_____

_____

_____

_____

One Thing Leads to Another

They said to him, "You're old, and your sons don't live as you do. Give us a king to rule over us like all the other nations." When the older leaders said that, Samuel was not pleased. He prayed to the LORD, and the LORD told Samuel, "Listen to whatever the people say to you. They have not rejected you. They have rejected me from being their king. They are doing as they have always done."

1 Samuel 8:5–8 NCV

The Big Picture

The Israelites were God's nation, called to the privilege of being ruled by God—a privilege they soon traded away.

Abraham's family grew numerous—just as God had promised. They became a nation, and were nearly destroyed by Egypt's pharaohs, but God saved them. As the people escaped Egypt, they recognized God as their King who would go behind and before them, lead and protect them.

But the Israelites proved to be a fickle people. They soon turned their attention to gods created in their minds, fashioned by their own hands. God sent leaders like Moses and Joshua to guide them back toward trusting him. He helped them select leaders to serve as judges, but the people still complained and sought a different way. The times were marked with disunity among their own, and wars with others. God predicted they would one day desire a king like other nations. For the Israelites, God—the Ruler of the universe—was not enough.

take a CLOSER look for women

The day finally came when they demanded an earthly king. For many years, Samuel had served as a judge to help rule the people as God directed. The elders of the tribes approached him. "You are old," they told him. "And your two sons are swindlers, not suitable to rule us. Appoint a king."

Samuel could see that their hearts were blinded. They had lost sight of God as the best king they could have. Samuel prayed, and God answered. "They have rejected me, not you. As usual, they serve other gods, and abandon me as their ruler." God told Samuel what to do. "Go ahead and do what they ask, but warn them what it's like to have kings like other nations."

Samuel told the Israelites that an earthly king could be tyrannical, and would take what they own—even their daughters. "You won't be able to cry out to God when this happens," he told them. They didn't care. They wanted someone—the sooner the better—to rule them, protect them, and lead them successfully through battles.

God directed Samuel to anoint a king. It launched an unsettling period of earthly reign. They had a few good rulers who served God and the nation well, but more who ruined the land through their unwise and immoral reigns. God kept a loving watch over Israel. He had a plan for this nation, and would never turn his back on them.

Either we are adrift in chaos or we are individuals, created, loved, upheld, and placed purposefully, exactly where we are. Can you believe that? Can you trust God for that?

Elisabeth Elliot

You already have the diamond necklace, but you'd rather wear one made of plastic beads. Sounds crazy, but that's about what the Israelites did. They had God as their ruler, and still an earthly king seemed like the answer to their problems. It started as a thought, grew into an attitude, and one thing led to another.

God said, "They are doing as they have always done." The Israelites had a history of forgetting God's powerful rule and protection. They regularly turned to worship other gods, and often had to be reminded to look back to God, who had seen them through many troubles.

And now, although it was against God's clear instructions, they sought a king who could rule over them and lead them victoriously through battles. Samuel had led them well up to that point, but the people felt they couldn't trust an aging man, or his wayward sons, to help them.

An earthbound mind-set led them through a series of choices that took them further and further away from the God who loved them. Instead of remembering the years of his steady care, they settled for a fallible source. Still, though they abandoned God, he would not abandon them.

> *Oh! If your heart swims in the rays of God's love, like a little mote swimming in the sunbeam, you will have no room in your heart for idols.*
>
> Robert Murray M'Cheyne

God created you to enjoy being a woman, and to have a place in your heart that is best filled by knowing him well. He designed your path to be an expression of your unique interests, talents, and personality, and at the same time, to unfold most beautifully within a trusting relationship with him.

He also hoped for a similar relationship with the Israelites. Unfortunately, they tended to pull out of God's arms into a place where they settled for less than his best. They did what they had done before. They forgot God's presence and love and, in fear, turned to earthly solutions to their dilemmas.

As you step into your day, think of what you find yourself trusting most: your abilities, intelligence, or beauty; other people, the media, or popular thought. Something guides your decisions. Consider what will take you closer to God's best for you. He allows you to go your own way, but he knows some choices can hurt you, and it breaks his heart.

Get to know God well. Catch a vision for his best, and never lose sight of it.

Now determine in your mind and heart to seek the LORD your God.

1 Chronicles 22:19 HCSB

The Israelites became impatient and blinded to the good they had in God as their King. Matthew Henry talked about this in his commentary:

"God designed them a king, a man after his own heart, when Samuel was dead; but they would anticipate God's counsel, and would have one now that Samuel was old. They had a prophet to judge them that had immediate correspondence with heaven, and therein they were great and happy above any nation, none having God so nigh unto them as they had."

The Israelites struggled much like people do today—with wanting something everyone else seemed to have. You can see this in the following excerpt from *John Gill's Exposition of the Entire Bible:*

"What they were desirous of was to have a king appearing in pomp and splendour, wearing a crown of gold, clothed in royal apparel, with a sceptre in his hand, dwelling in a stately palace, keeping a splendid court, and attended with a grand retinue, as the rest of the nations about them had had for a long time. . . . Israel had God for their King. . . . Happy it would have been for them if they had been content therewith.

Zooming **In**

The Ammonites were one of the nations the Israelites feared. In 1999, archaeologists discovered a seal of an Ammonite king mentioned in the Bible. His name was Ba'alis. The tiny seal is only 0.5" in diameter and 0.2" thick. It is made of brown agate, and has three lines of detailed script indicating its ownership.

The courts of Israel had an officer called a "recorder." He brought to the attention of the king the complaints and petitions of subjects or foreigners. As the royal historiographer, he recorded history, drafted treaties, and protected the national archives. For centuries, England has had a similar officer called a "remembrancer."

Consider how God uniquely designed you as an individual and as a woman. How might you use that uniqueness to know God better and stay close to him?

_____

_____

_____

_____

A threatening situation caused the Israelites to scramble for a king. How do you react to chaos? What purposeful steps might you take to trust, and involve, God's settling hand?

_____

_____

_____

Remembering is an important part of choosing God's best for each day. Consider the history of God's loving path for your life. What do you see?

_____

_____

_____

_____

Just Simple and Ordinary

As they observed the confidence of Peter and John and understood that they were uneducated and untrained men, they were amazed, and began to recognize them as having been with Jesus. And seeing the man who had been healed standing with them, they had nothing to say in reply.

Acts 4:13–14 NASB

The Big Picture

What an amazing time in history to be a part of. Jesus had died and miraculously come back to life. For forty days he walked among his friends, ate with them, and taught them. Many saw him, even touched him. Then he rose into the clouds. He promised that the Holy Spirit would give the apostles power to tell others about him and all that had happened.

One afternoon, while entering the temple complex in Jerusalem, Peter and John encouraged a lame man to stand: "In the name of Jesus Christ, get up off the ground and walk." The man took Peter's hand and stood as the crowd watched. Many ran toward them, and Peter began to speak. "Why are you so amazed?" he asked them. He reminded them of the power of faith, and invited them to think about Jesus: "God gave you his Son, Jesus. Do you see he sent him to bless you? Please don't continue your rebellious ways."

Also in the crowd were the temple priests and the temple guard. So were the Sadducees, a Jewish sect who adamantly denied the resurrection of

take a CLOSER look for women

Jesus. These groups included men who hated Jesus and what he preached. They hoped nailing him to a cross would bring an end to his teachings. It clearly hadn't.

Incensed, these men pushed through the crowds to confront Peter and John. It was too late in the day to gather the council. They took them into custody. The next day, Peter and John went before the chief priests and elders. The healed man was also there. The council asked the apostles, "By what authority did you cure this man?"

Inspired by the Holy Spirit, Peter addressed the council. He spoke with clarity and boldness as he defended his actions, shared about Jesus, and explained fulfilled prophecy. The council was astonished by the poise with which the men spoke. They detected a note of authority, which they found unusual for Peter's and John's lack of training. Clearly these two had spent time with Jesus. They would not charge them, but they demanded that they stop preaching about Jesus.

God's Spirit was with Peter and John, and they remained bold: "You decide if it's right or wrong in God's sight for us to listen to you," they told the council. "We cannot stop speaking about all that has happened."

You have given up your old way of life with its habits. Each of you is now a new person. You are becoming more and more like your Creator, and you will understand him better.

Colossians 3:9–10 CEV

Spend time with a wise and gracious woman, and you might find her character rubbing off on you. Look what happened to two uneducated fishermen who spent time with Jesus. They ended up amazing the religious leaders with their confidence and boldness.

The leaders knew enough about Peter and John to realize that they had not had the same educational opportunities they had. How could they speak so wisely and courageously? As Peter and John spoke, the Jewish leaders remembered the many times they had heard Jesus speak. They did not like what he did or taught, but they had become well acquainted with his ability to confidently respond to their questions. With quiet authority, he spoke about the history, prophecies, and law that the Jewish leaders had learned through ardent training. He calmly challenged them. So did Peter and John.

The leaders tried to understand, but could only conclude that the men learned their boldness by being around Jesus. They couldn't see the deeper, powerful work of the Holy Spirit as Peter and John spoke. That, too, was the glorious expression of having spent time with Jesus.

> *Prayer involves transformed passions. In prayer, real prayer, we begin to think God's thoughts after Him: to desire the things He desires, to love the things He loves, to will the things He wills.*
>
> Richard J. Foster

A beginning quilter spends time with an expert quilter, watching the aged but nimble fingers quickly glide the needle in and out of the fabric layers. Shaky at first, her confidence grows, and she, too, learns the rhythm of the needle.

Apply It
to Your Life

Jesus invites you to take his hand so you can explore the paths of his heart and life. Spend time with him—through reading about him in the Bible, and through prayer. Others will begin to recognize you as having been with Jesus.

Read about Jesus' life. Walk down the Jerusalem streets and explore the Galilean towns with him. Notice how he prayed, how he loved, how he cried. See how he fought for people's hearts, how he hoped for the best for each one he met. Begin to pray, love, and cry as he did. Hope. That's spending time with Jesus.

When you begin to do that, image doesn't matter so much—neither the one you wish you had, nor the one you struggle to maintain. You can stand before others confidently, and trust what God has placed inside you, no matter what others think.

Because Peter and John had been with Jesus, they trusted that God could accomplish the extraordinary through them. Spend time with Jesus, and watch him accomplish the extraordinary through you.

All of us, then, reflect the glory of the Lord with uncovered faces; and that same glory, coming from the Lord, who is the Spirit, transforms us into his likeness in an ever greater degree of glory.

2 Corinthians 3:18 GNT

Ray Stedman, in his Expository Studies in Acts sermon series, commented on how the Jewish leaders might have viewed spending time with Jesus:

"They had noted that . . . [Jesus] evidenced a remarkable poise; nothing they said or did to him ever seemed to trouble him. Here were men who were reflecting the same spirit. They had doubtless become aware of the fact that anyone who had anything to do with Jesus for very long began to act differently—he became a different person, and manifested an obvious confidence, an air of boldness and quiet authority."

Being with Jesus transformed Peter and John. Steve Zeisler discussed how this happened in his sermon "Obeying Men or God":

"They had listened to him, traveled with him, and watched him die. By the witness of the Spirit they had now come to understand the things he taught. Being with Jesus makes a person courageous, wise, humble, sensitive, and strong. And we have the option of being with Jesus as much as they did. . . . We can listen, actively seek him out, long to learn from him, and apply the lessons he taught."

Zooming **In**

In ancient times, authoritative teachers of the law given by Moses were called *ribbi*, meaning "teacher," or "great one." These teachers were appointed to be the religious leaders of their communities. Today the common term is *rabbi*. Orthodox Jews consider Moses to be the first rabbi. He passed on the leadership of this office to Joshua in an "ordination," or "laying of hands," called *semicha*. By tradition, the authority of *semicha* is transferred from one rabbi to another, and this has continued from Moses' time to the present day. An individual obtains *semicha* only after completing rigorous studies in Jewish law and literature.

Peter and John spent several years with Jesus watching him live. They loved Jesus so much that his work became theirs. So did his boldness. A relationship with Jesus does that.

Jesus made it a point to spend intimate time with people. He still does. What will you ask him about his life, and the way he lived boldly?

_____

_____

_____

_____

God sees your image as a woman as one who can speak boldly of his work in your life. Describe what your life will look like as you spend more time with him.

_____

_____

_____

_____

It takes time to know God well, and to begin to reflect his character in your life. Be patient. What specific characteristics would you like to see growing stronger today?

_____

_____

_____

A Mysterious Reminder

I don't want anyone to think more highly of me than what they can actually see in my life and my message, even though I have received wonderful revelations from God. But to keep me from getting puffed up, I was given a thorn in my flesh.

2 Corinthians 12:6–7 NLT

The Big Picture

Like ripples in a pond, teachings about Christ and his forgiveness spread out from Jerusalem, north to Turkey, across Asia, and into Macedonia. A man whose name meant "little" helped launch this important time in history. His name was Paul (or you might call him Saul), and it was the first century.

Paul was small but feisty. A Jew by birth, he was well versed in Old Testament and rabbinical teachings. At first, when the numbers of Jesus' followers grew, Paul's fury increased in proportion. He raced through the countryside to stop the spread; even murder would be justified.

On one of those trips, Jesus appeared to Paul. That encounter changed him forever. His zeal would now be spent helping the message about Jesus go farther than anyone had thought possible. He journeyed into the lands around the Mediterranean Sea and established many new churches. He also faced difficulties, including imprisonment and violent persecution.

On his third journey, he traveled his farthest yet—to Macedonia, or Greece. One bustling trade center he visited was Corinth, a wealthy harbor city steeped in immorality and the worship of gods. Paul, a tentmaker by trade, stayed with a couple, Aquila and Priscilla, who were also tentmakers. Paul worked diligently alongside them, and they helped him begin a new church in Corinth.

After a year and a half, Paul continued his journeys. While he traveled, he wrote several letters to the Corinthian church to encourage and caution them. The believers there seemed to easily suffer from divisiveness and teachers who led them astray. Some spread lies about Paul and successfully undermined his authority. Many at the Corinthian church began to doubt Paul's integrity.

Heartbroken, Paul wrote a very personal letter to the Corinthians. He reminded them of his reliability. Though he may not have been eloquent, he had taught them well. Because men had come among them claiming to have special visions, he cautioned about their intentions. In doing so, he spoke of humility and weaknesses, especially as they applied to his life. He had received generous revelations from God, but had been careful about telling them—just in case anyone considered him greater than he really was. "In fact," he told them, "to keep me humble, I have been given a thorn in my flesh."

Paul had asked God many times to remove this thorn, but he didn't. Sometimes, even with prayer, difficulties remain. Paul trusted that his had a purpose.

Adversity is the diamond dust heaven polishes its jewels with.

Robert Leighton

Paul had plenty to boast about, and probably struggled with pride as easily as anyone. To help in that, he said he was given a thorn in his flesh. Notice that his letter never specified what this "thorn" was. The mysteriousness of Paul's thorn makes it possible for others like you to say, "I know what he felt like. I have a 'thorn,' too."

In Greek, *thorn* is *skolops*—something pointed and sharp that causes severe pain and is a constant irritation. It wasn't a rose thorn. Paul, a tent-maker, more likely considered it similar to a tent stake. It might have been a severe limitation, or illness, or any number of difficulties, but it is left undefined.

Those who knew Paul may have been very aware of what he meant. For them, and future readers, he helps them see it differently: Paul said that his thorn was "given" to him. It was a gift given—a welcomed reminder—to keep him humble. Though painful, Paul viewed it as an opportunity to trust God more. With his thorn, he would never be mistaken about the source of the power, or the grace, to move forward in his journeys.

> Oh, there must be the weakness of man, felt, recognized, and mourned over, or else the strength of the Son of God will never be perfected in us.
>
> Charles Spurgeon

You might have a "thorn" that is a painful and constant irritation. It hinders. It brings you to your knees in frustration. The way it pricks your life causes far deeper sorrow than any rose thorn could.

God, who directed every word that would be in the Bible, knew the specificity of Paul's thorn would be absent—because he thought of you. Your thorn would be different from Paul's.

What information did God include instead? A reminder that he has given you delightful opportunities that came only from him. A reminder that your limitations can be beautifully supplied through his power and graciousness. And yes, a reminder that your thorn is a gift—something that can be used well.

Don't let your thorn stop you from pursuing all that God has for you. Look for the ways it helps put into perspective who you are before God. You are a woman he created lovely, and for a purpose. Through the unique gift of your thorn, you can daily reveal God's beauty and power.

In certain ways we are weak, but the Spirit is here to help us. For example, when we don't know what to pray for, the Spirit prays for us in ways that cannot be put into words.

Romans 8:26 CEV

Weakness and difficulties are often seen as thorns. John Piper, in his sermon "Christ's Power Made Perfect in Weakness," encouraged those who struggled:

"The deepest need that you and I have in weakness and adversity is not quick relief, but the well-grounded confidence that what is happening to us is part of the greatest purpose of God in the universe—the glorification of the grace and power of his Son—the grace and power that bore him to the cross and kept him there until the work of love was done.

"Paul asked for his thorn to be removed. When it wasn't, he learned an important lesson."

This is discussed in the May 27, 1998, devotional in Moody Bible Institute's *Today in the Word*:

"One paradox of the Christian life is that we discover our greatest spiritual power when we admit our total inability to do anything in our strength. God taught Paul this lesson through his distressing problem. So the issue for Paul was this: Did he want relief more than he wanted God's power? Did he hunger for peaceful circumstances more than he hungered for spiritual strength? Paul's answer rings out: 'I delight in [my] weaknesses.'"

Zooming In

Paul's thorn was figurative, but real, in its affliction on his life. Palestine, however, did have famous "thorn" plants. The zizypus and the Palestine buckthorn were two of the most well known in biblical times. They were often planted purposely and used as hedges. The buckthorn worked well as firewood for cooking meat.

Poseidon, god of the seas and earthquakes, held great significance for Corinth, the popular seaport Paul visited. In myths, Poseidon often displayed a bad temper. As "Earth shaker," he controlled the seas through violent earthquakes. His name was common in Greek literature and poetry. One popular work is Homer's *Odyssey*.

Paul's thorn remains a mystery to readers today. You, on the other hand, are well acquainted with your thorn, and its pain and inconvenience. Could God have a purpose for yours too?

Through the
Eyes of
Your Heart

You are like a rose. Though it has thorns, it has beauty and fragrance. How can you begin to find the beauty in having your thorn? What is one thing you see in it that encourages you?

_____

_____

_____

Paul was an intelligent and gifted man. His thorn helped him to see God's hand in what he accomplished. Where do you see God in the gifts and abilities you have?

_____

_____

_____

Even with, and maybe especially with, your thorn, you have wonderful opportunities ahead. Dream. What are the ways God might powerfully use you *because* of your thorn?

_____

_____

_____

A Matter of the Heart

The Big Picture

"People judge others by what they see on the outside, but God looks at the heart," God once told his prophet Samuel. A king's heart was important to God; it could influence an entire nation.

In Judah, Israel's Southern Kingdom, it was customary for a son to succeed his father. All of Judah's kings were descendants of King David. Over and over the Bible speaks of the heart of these men. Some were good, and others were very evil. Descriptions ranged from "his heart delighted in God's ways," to "his actions were evil because he refused to set his heart to seek God."

One day an eight-year-old named Josiah became king when his father was assassinated. Both his father and grandfather were bad kings. Somehow, in spite of his heritage and his father's example, young King Josiah had a heart for God. He had much to learn, but he did all he could to please God and reign well.

When he was twenty-six years old, he decided to rebuild God's temple, for it had been destroyed by his grandfather's sordid use of it. Josiah sent his secretary, Shaphan, to request funds from the high priest, Hilkiah. The priest informed Shaphan that he had found the Book of the Law in the temple. Shaphan returned to the king, and reported that the temple rebuilding would begin as requested. He also read the Book of the Law to Josiah.

As Josiah listened, he realized how prior kings had turned their back on God and degraded the worship practices. He tore his robes in fear and grief. "Surely God is outraged by our hard-hearted disobedience to his law." Judah deserved punishment, and Josiah sought to know what God would do.

Yes, God was angry. Judah's disobedience under the rule of the evil kings had put the country in a state of chaos and immorality. They would face consequences. But God said to Josiah, "Your heart is tender and humble. I have heard you." Judah would experience peace during Josiah's reign.

King Josiah renewed a covenant with God, and spent the remainder of his reign rebuilding the temple and reforming Judah. He purged the land of idols and all occult and immoral practices. In the end it was said of Josiah, "Never has there been and never will there be a king like Josiah who turned totally to God and obeyed with all his heart, soul, and strength."

The word of God hidden in the heart is a stubborn voice to suppress.

Billy Graham

Often, as women, we may feel as if we need a total makeover. Yet sometimes what is really needed is a heart makeover. That's what happened to Josiah. Hearing God's words moved him so profoundly that he realized he and his nation were looking pretty shabby—mostly on the inside. Notice that his makeover went deep, to the heart level, encompassing all that he had thought, and all he did. It was total.

As soon as Josiah understood how far Judah had strayed into evil, he "turned" to God. The Hebrew word *shub* means "to go back, to reestablish." It carries with it the idea of a repentant and obedient heart, which Josiah certainly displayed. This change in his heart guided his future actions, which included respecting every word of God's law.

From that moment forward, Josiah's devotion to God, and to leading his kingdom well, became passionate, sincere, and steady. So much so that he launched a zealous crusade. He strove to bring God back, not only into every corner of his life, but also to every corner of the kingdom. He reestablished conscious living for God's purposes. He was on fire—inspired by God, and longing to light that flame in the hearts of everyone in his kingdom. Now that's a total makeover.

> *Always seek peace between your heart and God, but in this world, always be careful to remain ever-restless, never satisfied, and always abounding in the work of the Lord.*
>
> Jim Elliot

You, as a woman, will find yourself in many different positions of leadership throughout your life. You may lead a few individuals or many. At times you may guide quietly. Other times you will visibly be the one to look up to. Your leadership might be within the community, a family, a job, or a ministry—roles God uniquely intended for you.

Apply It
to Your Life

Josiah stood out in sharp contrast to the kings before him. Instead of destruction, he built up. Instead of being self-focused, he was God-focused. Instead of denying God's law, he honored it. Each of his actions helped bring back some of the restoration, growth, and health that God desired for Judah. And it all began with Josiah, and a moment of choosing to turn his heart passionately toward God.

Josiah provided a magnificent example. To be a worthy leader, you begin at the heart level. He led with humility, and total loyalty, to God and his words. You may have found as you have grown in your devotion toward God that you've had a stronger desire to include his instructions for you in all areas of your life, including how you lead others. What a beautiful opportunity you have to lead well.

Love the Lord your God with all your heart, with all your soul, with all your mind, and with all your strength.

Mark 12:30 GNT

Josiah loved God's law, and he showed it in all of his actions. E. M. Bounds, in *The Necessity of Prayer,* noted how important God's words were to Josiah:

"With this righteous king, God's Word was of great importance. He esteemed it at its proper worth, and counted a knowledge of it to be of such grave importance, as to demand his consulting God in prayer about it, and to warrant the gathering together of the notables of his kingdom, so that they, together with himself, should be instructed out of God's book concerning God's law."

Matthew Henry, in his *Commentary of the Whole Bible,* talked about some of the characteristics that made Josiah one of the best kings. Henry encouraged his readers to live likewise:

"That he did it with all his heart, and all his soul, and all his might—with vigour, and courage, and resolution: he could not otherwise have broken through the difficulties he had to grapple with. What great things may we bring to pass in the service of God if we be but lively and hearty in it!"

Zooming **In**

God's law is part of what is called the *Torah,* or "a teaching," which is made up of the first five books of the Old Testament. Today Jewish scribes handwrite the Torah in Hebrew calligraphy on parchment scrolls. When read during a service, the reader avoids touching the paper, and instead, uses a pointer called a *Yad,* which means "hand" in Hebrew.

The Wailing Wall in Jerusalem is known by Jews as the Western Wall, or *Kotel* in Hebrew. This wall is all that's left of the temple Josiah had reestablished. It is the temple that Solomon built, which was destroyed in AD 70. Considered the most holy site for Judaism, it is still a traditional place for daily prayer.

Josiah proved to be a leader who reigned with his heart set toward God. What a dynamic way to carry out God's leadership roles for you as a woman.

Through the
Eyes of
Your Heart

Heritage doesn't matter as Josiah showed. It's a heart choice to lead well. What do you feel you have to overcome? How can God help you do that?

_____

_____

_____

_____

Josiah's leadership skills grew as he better understood God's ways. What of God's ways would you like to learn more about? How will learning this change how you lead?

_____

_____

_____

Spiritual restoration and growth were an important part of Josiah's goals for Judah. What goals has God given you in your areas of leadership? Do you now see a few new goals?

_____

_____

_____

I'm Listening

Samuel did not yet know the LORD, and the word of the LORD had not yet been revealed to him. The LORD called Samuel again, a third time. And he got up and went to Eli, and said, "Here I am, for you called me." Then Eli perceived that the LORD was calling the boy. Therefore Eli said to Samuel, "Go, lie down; and if he calls you, you shall say, 'Speak, LORD, for your servant is listening.'"

1 Samuel 3:7–9 NRSV

The Big Picture

Samuel was just a small boy when he came to live in God's temple with Eli, the high priest. The boy's mother had promised God that her son would live his life serving him with the priests. Every year she visited during the festivals. He knew she loved him. He could see it in her eyes as she draped a priestly coat across his shoulders, a coat she had woven herself.

Though he lived with priests, he really wasn't one himself. Eli's sons were—but barely. They spurned God and lived corrupt lives. Eli refused to discipline them. The aging priest would pay dearly for that leniency. He did better with Samuel. He sensed that God was preparing this boy for a special role in Israel's history.

Samuel grew strong and wise. He learned about God and desired to serve him. Living with the priests, he heard stories about how the Holy One spoke to people directly, or in visions. At that time, however, God spoke only rarely.

One night, when Samuel was twelve years old, he went to his bed in the

take a CLOSER look for women

temple. The golden lampstand nearby was lit, and the glow of its burning oil softened the dark night. Eli slept in another room close by. As Samuel lay down to sleep, a voice broke through the quiet. Samuel answered, "I'm here." He arose and went to Eli's room. "Here I am."

"I didn't call you," Eli told him. "Go back to sleep."

Samuel lay down and heard the voice again: "Samuel." Again he went to Eli.

"I didn't call you, son," Eli assured Samuel.

It happened once more. This time Eli knew it must be God. "Go back and lie down. Answer if you hear the voice again. Say to God, 'Speak, Lord. I'm your servant, and I'm listening.'"

Samuel returned to his bed. Soon he heard the voice say, "Samuel, Samuel." Samuel realized that God must be there with him, and he answered, "Speak. Your servant is listening."

Over the next moments God talked with young Samuel, giving him warnings and instructions to share with Eli. God was not pleased with Eli's service or his handling of his sons. It would be a difficult message to give, but God was preparing Samuel to step into his new role as his prophet. He would become well acquainted with God's voice.

I wait for the LORD, my soul waits, and in His word I do hope. My soul waits for the Lord more than those who watch for the morning—yes, more than those who watch for the morning.

Psalm 130:5–6 NKJV

Journaling brings you into a quiet place where you can hear your own thoughts. Sometimes in those moments, you also hear God. How amazing it must have been to hear God's voice as Samuel did. Notice his readiness to respond, even before he knew it was God.

In Samuel's time the Israelites had once again turned their back on God. Their hearts were hard, even those within the priesthood, and they did not seek God's voice. Yet God was present. He would speak and give guidance to those who honestly sought him.

He did not know God well, but Samuel's heart was wide open to serve. When he didn't recognize God's voice, the young boy still responded with a willingness to be available. He ran to discover the need and said, "I am here."

Once Eli realized it was God, he gave Samuel instructions on how to be available to God. Go lie down—go wait for him. *If* God speaks again—for it is up to him—*then* respond with humility: "I am your servant. I am listening." Samuel did. His heart truly was open and ready to hear what God would tell his servant.

> *[God] brings me into a relationship with Himself where I hear His call and understand what He wants me to do, and I do it out of sheer love to Him.*
>
> Oswald Chambers

God designed you, a woman, to be sensitive to the needs around you. It would be against your nature to ignore them. Yes, sometimes you are not able to respond, but the need still tugs at your soul. When you are able to help, the way you choose to fill that need is distinctive, and reflects your personality and womanhood.

Apply It
to Your Life

God speaks through the Bible. Through his words, you hear his whispers. They show you his heart. They tell you how he loves you, and how he wants you to love others. But God also speaks through the uniqueness of how he made you. None of that is by chance. Your sensitivities, your longings, what moves you to tears or makes you laugh, can be ways in which God speaks particularly to you.

God created, within you, a spiritual heart, which can be fine-tuned to hear his whisperings. He desires for you to know him, to become well acquainted with his voice. You only need to be like Samuel, available to listen and respond when he speaks: "Hear I am, Lover of my Soul. I am available to you, and I am listening."

A voice came out of the cloud, saying, "This is My Son, My Chosen One; listen to Him!"

Luke 9:35 NASB

Many wonder how God spoke to people, or how he might speak today. James M. Gray, in *The Concise Bible Commentary*, addressed this question:

"How God spake to Samuel we are not informed, but His voice in earlier times was heard in a literal sense, and there is no good reason to doubt that it was here. Of course, God is not a man with physical organs, but who shall say that He who made man's voice is not able Himself to be heard and understood by man?"

Even as you read God's words in the Bible, you can respond to him. David Guzik, in his Enduring Word Commentary series, talked about Samuel's ready response to God:

"Samuel was so impressed by what he heard, he responded by saying, Here I am! What a beautiful way to respond to God's Word! It isn't that God does not know where we are before we tell Him, but it tells God and it reminds us we are simply before Him as servants, asking what He wants us to do."

Zooming **In**

The priests wore a "robe of the ephod," which was blue, sleeveless, and woven without a seam. It was worn over a simple undergarment that had sleeves. The skirt was trimmed with colorful pomegranates, and a gold bell between each. Samuel's mother might have woven a similar robe for her son.

The golden lampstand, near where Samuel slept, was just outside the most holy place in the temple. Its central stand branched out at the top to hold seven lamps that burned olive oil. The lampstand was made out of a solid block of gold, and weighed one talent, or about seventy-five pounds. The estimated worth in gold today would be half a million dollars.

Samuel was only beginning to recognize God's voice, but he had the heart attitude that made him available to listen. You can learn to hear God's whispers, too.

Through the
Eyes of
Your Heart

Sometimes God's voice comes within a thought, recognized by its clarity and wisdom. If it is consistent with what the Bible says, listen. In what ways have you heard God?

_____

_____

_____

Another way to listen to God is to allow him to use the natural abilities you have as a woman to see the needs around you. How can he uniquely use you in these situations?

_____

_____

_____

Maybe what you need to hear most in God's whisperings is how special you are to him. Write a prayer letter to him. What do you hear from him in response?

_____

_____

_____

_____

You Can Do It

When Sanballat, Tobiah, and Geshem the Arab heard of our plan, they scoffed contemptuously. "What are you doing, rebelling against the king like this?" they asked. But I replied, "The God of heaven will help us succeed. We his servants will start rebuilding this wall."

Nehemiah 2:19–20 NLT

The
Big Picture

Passionate, loyal, determined—that was Nehemiah. He was a Jew born in captivity, and the trusted courtier in the service of a Persian king. God had plans for this person of character.

Babylon had stormed Judah, burned Jerusalem, and captured the Israelites. The Hebrews lived in exile for more than 150 years. They longed to return to Jerusalem to rebuild. After Persia conquered Babylon, King Cyrus allowed some to go back, and they rebuilt the temple. Later more returned. Slowly, the Hebrews began to reclaim their way of life.

Nehemiah worked as a cupbearer in the courts of a later king, Artaxerxes. He served wine at the king's table and was considered a trusted adviser. One day, a dear Hebrew brother visited from Jerusalem. He told Nehemiah how broken down the city was. The gates and the walls were still lying in rubble from the invasion.

Nehemiah's heart was broken. He wept, prayed, and fasted for several months. He told God, "Surely we are ready to be faithful to you. Help us return to our land."

One day, as Nehemiah served wine, the king noticed his sadness. "What's wrong?" he asked.

Though afraid he might insult the king, Nehemiah answered. "May the king live forever," he began, "but how can I be happy when my ancestors' city lies in ruins?"

"What would you do?"

Nehemiah silently thanked God for the king's openness. "If I have your favor, please send me to the land of my fathers so that I may help rebuild it."

The king granted Nehemiah permission, and provided letters to assure safe passage in his travels to Jerusalem. On the way, Nehemiah could gather needed lumber from the king's forest.

When Nehemiah arrived in Jerusalem, he took a few men and quietly surveyed the city gates and walls. Next, he requested the support of the Jewish officials and priests. "God has graciously made every step possible, even securing the favor of the king."

These leaders supported Nehemiah, but others sought to thwart his efforts. Three foreigners, Sanballat, Tobiah, and Geshem, mocked him. "You can't do this. We doubt you have the king's permission."

Nehemiah had more than the king's permission. "It is God who will give us success," he told them. "We serve him, and will rebuild." In spite of further opposition, including threats on his life, Nehemiah and his workers forged ahead and rebuilt the wall. God granted success. The entire wall, several miles in length, was rebuilt in fifty-two days.

Trust the LORD with all your heart, and don't depend on your own understanding. Remember the LORD in all you do, and he will give you success.

Proverbs 3:5–6 NCV

Maybe you've redecorated a room, even tackled a remodel. Imagine facing a renovation of an entire city. Nehemiah just wanted to work on the walls, but that proved to be difficult, even with King Artaxerxes' help. Notice that Nehemiah forged ahead because he had the best authority to succeed—God's.

The three foreigners tried to undermine the project, but Nehemiah stood firm. What was behind his confidence? At first glace, it seems it would be the authority of the Persian king. After all, Nehemiah possessed the finances, materials, and letters of authority his taunters claimed he didn't have. How easy it would have been to silence them with that proof. But Nehemiah didn't. Instead he told them, "God will help us succeed," and "We his servants will rebuild."

As much as Nehemiah appreciated the support of the Persian king, that meant little compared to the authority of God—the King of kings. In fact, he spent months talking to God before he approached the king. He wouldn't have moved forward without God. He was that kind of person. So, in the face of threats, he could confidently answer by whose authority he would rebuild—and by whose he would succeed.

> *Hope does not necessarily take the form of excessive confidence; rather, it involves the simple willingness to take the next step.*
>
> Stanley Hauerwas

A grapevine wreath is constructed and shaped one vine at a time. Each of those vines has been cured and strengthened before it is used. It takes time, but once the wreath is completed, it will last almost forever. Dreams and goals are a little like that.

Sometimes you give a dream your all, and the progress seems so slow. Doubt stirs. Others suggest you give it up. What do you do? Remember the grapevine wreath—one vine at a time. Be patient. If the dream is God's goal for you, and you know it, like Nehemiah, you hang on with every tenacious bone in your body. Don't let others stop you. Pray and ask God to show you the possibilities. Gather those around you who will help you move forward.

And watch out for inner discouragement. Sometimes *you* can be your worst enemy. You look for the broken pieces within your dreams, and say it's no use. You taunt and tease, and make yourself believe you're not capable. Stop. Let God direct the progress of the goal and the direction it takes. Trust him. Talk to him—a lot. Then move ahead with confidence that he will help you succeed, one vine at a time.

God can do anything, you know—far more than you could ever imagine or guess or request in your wildest dreams! He does it not by pushing us around but by working within us, his Spirit deeply and gently within us.

Ephesians 3:20 MSG

Ray Stedman considered the symbolism of Nehemiah's rebuilding of Jerusalem's walls. In his sermon "Nehemiah: Rebuilding the Walls," he said:

"What does it mean, then, to rebuild the walls of your life? Nehemiah is the account of the rebuilding of the walls of Jerusalem. And Jerusalem is a symbol of the city of God, God's dwelling place, and the center of life for the world. In an individual life, then, the rebuilding of the walls would be a picture of reestablishing the strength of that life."

Prayer was important for Nehemiah in the face of his enemies. F. B. Meyer, in a devotion called "Religion and Ridicule" *in Daily Walk*, applied this to today:

"There is our up-look into God's face—'I prayed to the God of Heaven.' We must never forget to pray, for more things are wrought by prayer than we realize. Second, there is our up-look against our foes and the foes of God—'We made our prayer unto our God, and set a watch against them day and night.' We must watch as well as pray."

Zooming **In**

At the turn of the twentieth century, a clay cylinder was excavated in southern Iraq and eventually placed in a British museum. The cylinder, about 12" long, details King Cyrus's conquest of Babylon in 539 BC. It also tells about the release of the Judean captives: "I liberated those who dwelt in Babylon from the yoke that chafed them."

The ancient cities of the East all used massive walls for protection, including Jerusalem. Its high, thick walls were made of gray stone. In Jesus' time, the wall was about four miles in circumference. Those you see in Jerusalem today were built in the 1500s by a Turkish sultan, and are less than two miles in length.

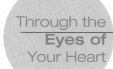
Once Nehemiah understood that God wanted him to rebuild the walls, nothing could deter him. Get God involved in your dreams, and watch what happens.

Do you have a dream? With a broken heart, Nehemiah prayed to God about Jerusalem. What passions stir your heart? What might God be telling you to do?

_____

_____

_____

In what way do you get easily discouraged about your goals? Do you do that to yourself? Do others do that? What's the next "vine" you'll add to confidently build your dream?

_____

_____

_____

Nehemiah recognized that he was God's servant, and God was behind his goals. How can you invite God into your dreams and the direction they will take? What would you ask him?

_____

_____

_____

With Open Arms

Joseph said to his brothers, "Please, come near me,"
and they came near. "I am Joseph, your brother," he
said, "the one you sold into Egypt. And now don't be
worried or angry with yourselves for selling me here,
because God sent me ahead of you to preserve life."

Genesis 45:4–5 HCSB

The
Big Picture

It was a nightmare. No matter what Joseph did, all his brothers, except Benjamin, despised him. Yes, Joseph was a favorite of his father. And maybe Joseph shouldn't have told his brothers his dreams of how they would someday bow to him. But those weren't good reasons to throw him into a pit, and leave him to starve. He could have died if it weren't for those traders. His brothers actually sold him. What would they tell their father? That he had been eaten by wild animals?

Living in Egypt turned out okay, except for one patch of jail time. A captain bought Joseph and made him a trusted servant of his household, but then he was falsely accused and imprisoned. After several years in prison, Joseph earned pharaoh's trust by honestly interpreting his dreams. The nation would face a famine. The pharaoh honored Joseph by giving him authority over his household and nation. Joseph wisely prepared for the famine, and the nation was ready when it came.

Joseph watched as many from other countries poured into Egypt seeking food. One day his brothers arrived—all except Benjamin.

take a CLOSER look for women

They didn't recognize him, and at first he treated them harshly. He devised a way to see his youngest brother. First, he'd require one to stay while the rest took food back to the family. Then he'd make it seem as if they had kept money they owed. They'd have to return for their brother and be honest.

The brothers discovered the money and knew they had to return. Their father, Jacob, reluctantly let them take Benjamin. Joseph claimed God provided the money in their bags, and then sent them on their way again with a similar plan. This time he also put a silver cup in Benjamin's food bag. The one found with the cup would become his slave.

When Joseph's men discovered the cup, the brothers returned and begged Joseph not to take Benjamin. "How could we go home without him? Our father could not bear it."

Joseph began to weep. "I am Joseph," he confessed, but that revelation terrified his brothers.

"Please, come here," he told them. "Don't be afraid or mad at yourselves for selling me. It was God's plan that I come to Egypt. He sent me to help save lives." That was true. God used all that seemed to go wrong to position Joseph to save Egypt, and also his family—the beginning of the Hebrew nation of Israel.

Never does the human soul appear so strong and noble as when it forgoes revenge and dares to forgive an injury.

Edwin Hubbell Chapin

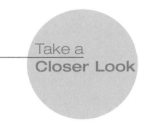

Betrayal rips the cloth of friendship and family; forgiveness sews it back together again.

Joseph's brothers betrayed him. He could easily have chosen to be angry and never forgive them. Instead, in an amazing show of compassion, he invited them to "please come near," *and* he urged them not to be afraid or angry with themselves.

By the time Joseph revealed his identity, his brothers had witnessed his position of power in Egypt. With one command, he might have made them slaves or had them killed—the very actions they had planned for him. Joseph was alive, and they were terrified. He asked them to come to him. It wasn't an order from a ruler; it was a plea from a loving brother. He longed for their nearness and a restoration of their relationship.

As they stepped forward, still doused in fear, Joseph spoke to them in self-less compassion. Most might say, *"I'm* not mad." He said, "Don't be mad at yourselves." Joseph had forgiven and put it all behind him; he wanted them to do the same.

This story is a wonderful picture of reconciliation. Joseph saw his place in God's plan for his family's preservation. God's forgiveness of his brothers became his own.

> *Forgiveness is the fragrance that the flower leaves on the heel of the one that crushed it.*
>
> Author Unknown

God's character is all about mending relationships, sewing the tattered edges back into wholeness—especially those where betrayal has torn so deep that repair seems impossible. Through Joseph's story, you see possibilities. You see hope.

It's difficult to know all that Joseph felt about his brothers up until that day he so thoroughly forgave them. Many years had passed. He might have felt overwhelmed with feelings of abandonment, grief, loneliness, and anger. You see him on the other side of those potentially dark years. Can you imagine what kind of person he would have been if the betrayal had consumed him? His well-being rested in his ability to trust God. In fact, his forgiveness was so crucial, it might have affected a nation's birth.

Your reactions to what has been done to you greatly affect your well-being. They also ripple through lives beyond your own. Your forgiveness. Your bitterness. Your love. Your hate. Your trust of God.

Climb into God's arms, dear daughter. Let him take the pain of the betrayal that has torn your heart. He knows what it feels like, and he has forgiven. He will gently show you how it's done.

When people sin, you should forgive and comfort them, so they won't give up in despair.

2 Corinthians 2:7 CEV

On May 11, 1862, Charles Spurgeon preached a sermon called "Joseph and the Brethren." He applied the image of Joseph's forgiveness to acceptance of God's forgiveness:

"What consolation Joseph gave! He did not say, 'I am not angry with you; I forgive you'; he said something sweeter than that—'Be not angry with yourselves,' as much as to say, 'As for me, ye need not question about that: be not grieved nor angry with yourselves.' So my blessed, my adorable Master says . . . 'My heart is made of tenderness, my bowels melt with love; forgive yourself.'"

Sometimes you are hurt by people who are acting out of their own hurts. John and Stasi Eldredge, in their book *Captivating*, tell how knowing that might help you forgive them:

"It might help to remember that those who hurt you were also deeply wounded themselves. They were broken hearts, broken when they were young, and they fell captive to the Enemy. . . . This doesn't absolve them of the choices they made, the things they did. It just helps us to let them go—to realize that they were shattered souls themselves.

Zooming **In**

To this day, archaeologists and historians struggle to reconcile Egyptian history with the story of Joseph. Still, there are some possible consistencies, particularly in the time of Sesostris I, the second king of the twelfth dynasty. In the tomb of one of the king's officers is an inscription: "No one was unhappy in my days, not even in the years of the famine." The message goes on to describe the gathering and storing of grain, and its distribution during a famine. The food was given freely, and without prejudice, to all who were hungry. The officer, whose name was Ameni, might have been one of Joseph's deputies.

Joseph longed to mend his relationship with his brothers. Look for those who need to hear you say, "Please come near."

Forgiveness doesn't excuse behavior, but it looks past it in hope. What are you finding difficult to forgive? Is there a way in which you can reach past it?

_____

_____

_____

_____

Joseph's brothers were terrified of him. Are those who might ask for your forgiveness afraid to approach you? How might you help them be more comfortable?

_____

_____

_____

_____

Joseph took the step to encourage his brothers not to be hard on themselves. When you are seeking forgiveness, can you forgive yourself? Do you believe God does?

_____

_____

_____

God, This Is a Tough One

> *I will climb up into my watchtower now and wait to see what the LORD will say to me and how he will answer my complaint. Then the LORD said to me, "Write my answer in large, clear letters on a tablet, so that a runner can read it and tell everyone else."*
>
> Habakkuk 2:1–2 NLT

The Big Picture

In Judah, the prophet Habakkuk faced a time not too unlike what you might read about in the daily newspaper—violence, greed, perverted justice, international crises. And he had questions for God, good questions.

Habakkuk watched the nation go from hope to disaster, from the reforms of the good King Josiah, to the corruption of King Jehoiakim. He knew God was holding back his chastisement of Israel only until the end of Josiah's life. The reign of the kings, descending from King David, was about to end. Judah's discipline was coming. The people wouldn't have known that, except God had warned them. Were they listening? Habakkuk was, and he wanted to talk to God about it.

"God, how long do I have to cry out to you for help, and you don't answer? Look at the violence and injustice in Judah. Why do you allow it? Troubles grow worse every day. The justice system isn't working. Judges twist the law to suit their needs. Why don't you do something about all this?"

God answered Habakkuk. "I have already planned to. Look at the reckless and terrible nation of Babylon. Their lawlessness can't be compared. They run over other nations with the swiftness of leopards and fierceness of wolves. Like eagles, they swoop and devour. They take men and women as captives—everyone in their path. Kings don't frighten them. They are proud of their strength. I will use Babylon to discipline Judah."

This stirred up more questions for the prophet. "You are the eternal and Holy God. I know you will not entirely destroy Judah, but you are good and just, and cannot endure their centuries of rebellion against you. And yet, I don't understand. You tolerate the evil of Babylon. Why? Are you going to stand by silently while they overtake Judah? Surely Judah is more righteous than they? Will Babylon get away with their actions?"

Then Habakkuk grew quiet. He said, "I will go to my watchtower and wait for God's answer."

God did answer, and he had much to say about Judah. Yes, at the right time Babylon would overtake them just as God had said. He told Habakkuk to write his response on a tablet in letters so large that a runner could read it and warn everyone.

This made Habakkuk tremble in fear, but he trusted God. He said, "I will take joy in God; he is my strength."

Faith waits and listens, knowing that in God's perfect time He will speak.

Kay Arthur

Like fragile china are people in the midst of disaster. Where is God? Does he care? Ask him.

Habakkuk courageously asked God the tough questions, but look closely at his manner. The way in which he framed the questions, plus his willingness to hear God's answers, showed he asked with worship and respect.

Habakkuk did not take his questions and complaints to God in pride, but in humble honesty. The nation's outright rebellion against God distressed Habakkuk, and God's reply pierced his heart with sorrow and dread. He had more questions for God.

When he finished his complaint, Habakkuk stopped to climb his watchtower. But did the prophet literally climb a tower? Prophets are often compared to alert and ready watchmen. Habakkuk stationed his heart to wait for God's answer. He prepared himself spiritually for what God would say. *Habakkuk* comes from the Hebrew word *habaq*, which means "to fold one's hands or embrace." The prophet would be humble and willing to embrace God's answer, even if he didn't fully understand it, even if it was difficult.

Habakkuk understood, and respected, God's nature and activity among his people. He understood the importance of God's just response to disobedience and lawlessness. He honored God and spoke with honesty, but reverence. God listened.

> *Though doubts and confusion reign when sin runs rampant, an encounter with God can turn those doubts into devotion and all confusion into confidence.*
>
> Ronald Blue

What is the cry of your heart? What do you long to hear from God? From Habakkuk you can learn a beautiful way to commune with God. He is approachable.

Apply It to Your Life

Habakkuk, the embracer and the embraced, felt confident in his relationship with God. He loved and honored God with all his heart, and God loved him. But Habakkuk still didn't always understand what God was doing—or not doing. So he asked. And then he listened.

Habakkuk discovered that though it looked as if God had been silent, he was working. He realized that even when God's plan included difficulty, it would be carried out by him whom Habakkuk could trust. Whatever happened, God would still be his source of joy and strength.

You are embraced by God. Lean into his arms with your questions, and then trust his silence as well as his answers. Let him help you find, in him, a joy that brightens the bleakest circumstances, and a strength that will carry you through the darkest nights. He is always with you, always willing to listen, and always trustworthy.

I will say to the LORD, "You are my refuge and my fortress, my God in whom I trust."

Psalm 91:2 GOD'S WORD

Habakkuk was willing to get quiet and hear God. In her study *Lord, Where Are You When Bad Things Happen?* Kay Arthur considered this and encouraged readers to learn to spend time with God:

"If you, too, will learn to wait upon God, to get alone with Him, and to remain silent so that you can hear His voice when He is ready to speak to you, what a difference it will make in your life! I think many of our problems overwhelm us simply because we do not set aside the time to be alone with God."

At first, Habakkuk thought God had been silent about the corruption in Judah. Charles L. Feinberg, in his book *The Minor Prophets,* considered how this applies to today:

"The silence of God in human affairs, then as now, has ever been difficult to understand. But this does not mean that there is not an answer, and that divine wisdom is incapable of coping with the situation. All is under His seeing eye, and everything is under the control of His mighty hand."

Zooming **In**

Watchmen were the alarm systems of ancient cities. These cities, along with their high, protective walls, used strategically positioned watchtowers. The towers provided a lookout point from which the watchmen could observe everything—all that went on within, and outside, the city gates. If he saw any sign of disturbances, intruders, or enemy attacks, he would sound an alarm.

Ancient tablets used for writing were rigid and flat and made out of many different kinds of materials: stone, clay, wood, bronze, lead, and gold. Many of these are mentioned in the Bible. The tablet, or *luach* in Hebrew, mentioned in Habakkuk, might have been made out of metal and raised on a building so that many could read it.

Habakkuk approached God with humility, and then asked the tough questions. God invites you, his daughter, to come and share the difficult questions you've wanted to ask.

Habakkuk made sure his heart was in the right place before he talked to God. What can you thank God for regarding who he is and what he's done? What about knowing him gives you joy?

_____

_____

_____

Much of what was happening in Habakkuk's day didn't make sense to him. He was concerned by the conditions around him. What doesn't make sense to you? Tell God.

_____

_____

_____

Habakkuk asked his questions then waited to see *if* God would answer. Can you trust him no matter what the answer? Journal about your growing trust in him.

_____

_____

_____

Let's Get Personal

Jesus stopped and told some people to bring the blind man over to him. When the blind man was getting near, Jesus asked, "What do you want me to do for you?" "Lord, I want to see!" he answered.

Luke 18:40–41 CEV

The Big Picture

"Here's our spot," Bartimaeus said as he tugged on his friend's hand. He pulled his blanket closer, then settled alongside the dusty Jericho road.

Both were blind. Through all kinds of weather they made their way to the streets to beg. They didn't have a choice, even though they knew, as Jews, this wasn't right. God's law made provisions for those in need, saying that there should be no poor among the Hebrews. The law was ignored. Bartimaeus and his friend were blind and poor. They begged to survive.

Often, as the two men sat, they heard conversations from those who passed—news of their neighbors and the marketplace, what was happening outside the gates of Jericho. They had also heard about Jesus. Bartimaeus believed he was the Son of David, the Messiah they had been waiting for. Perhaps he dreamed of the day Jesus would pass by their spot on the Jericho road. Well, one day he did.

It seemed to be a particularly busy day. Many were talking excitedly. Bartimaeus heard the scuffling of feet upon the road. "What's going on?" he asked. Someone responded, "Jesus of Nazareth is passing by."

take a CLOSER look for women

Jesus? He is here today? Bartimaeus's face lit up with excitement. How he wished he could see him. "Jesus!" he called out. "Have mercy on me."

Others hoped to catch a glimpse of Jesus too. One turned to Bartimaeus. "Be quiet, beggar."

Bartimaeus wanted his voice to be heard through the crowd. He tried again. "Son of David," he shouted louder, "please have mercy on me."

He heard someone say, "Bring him to me."

Bartimaeus felt hands lift him to his feet. "Get up. Jesus wants to see you." The blind man threw off his blanket and stumbled toward Jesus. He heard his kind voice say, "You asked for mercy. What do you wish for me to do?"

The Messiah. Bartimaeus could hardly contain his excitement. "Lord, I'd like to see."

Jesus answered him, "Have your sight. You asked in faith, and you shall be well."

Suddenly Bartimaeus could see, and the Messiah was standing right in front of him. Jesus began to move through the crowds. Bartimaeus followed him, overjoyed that God had made him well. Many recognized him as the blind beggar who now could see, and they thanked God too.

Jesus often healed physical ailments, but even more important to him was spiritual healing. Bartimaeus joyously received both.

Insomuch as any one pushes you nearer to God, he or she is your friend.

Author Unknown

Maybe you enjoy hosting parties—inviting and gathering people together, and encouraging new friendships. Jesus was like that too, but his parties happened everywhere, even in the streets of Jericho. Notice when Jesus healed Bartimaeus how he involved those around him to make it happen. God often acts within the context of relationships and community.

Bartimaeus had learned how to survive in his community. He was used to begging and being demeaned. "Be quiet, beggar," one had told him. Thankfully none of this stopped Bartimaeus from calling out to Jesus.

When Jesus stopped to respond, he got others involved. "Bring him to me," Jesus urged those nearby, maybe even the one who had told Bartimaeus to be quiet. Jesus then got Bartimaeus involved: "Tell me your need." The blind man's reply was a beautiful statement of faith that everyone heard. Honoring Jesus as God, he called him "Lord." The word in Greek is *kurios*, meaning "supreme authority or controller—Master, God." Bartimaeus knew who Jesus was and believed he could heal him, so he boldly stated his request for sight.

Jesus didn't throw out a quick healing and rush past. Each person lining that road mattered to him—the one who asked for mercy, and those nearby who needed to ask.

> *The vision must be followed by the venture. It is not enough to stare up the steps—we must step up the stairs.*
>
> Vance Havner

Hopefully you are in a community where you feel supported and encouraged, rather than left out and ignored. Perhaps you're waiting for Jesus to pass by. Speak up, and then get up. Jesus wants to see you.

What are you going to tell him as you stand face-to-face with him? He already knows the depths of your heart, the shape of each corner of your soul. He knows your body—every twisted muscle, broken bone, diseased cell. But he desires relationship. He wants involvement. Tell him your need.

When Bartimaeus told him his, he received a beautiful gift, and it wasn't just his sight. It was Jesus himself—God getting personal. Do you recognize Jesus as Bartimaeus did? Then call him "Lord," and believe that he is. When you meet Jesus face-to-face like that, it changes you.

Now look around your community. Look for other women who have hurt as you have—others who need someone to tell them they matter. Encourage them. Maybe even tell them, "Get up. Jesus wants to see you." Then give them a hand. Walk with them. Hold them up. Love them.

Love each other with genuine affection, and take delight in honoring each other.

Romans 12:10 NLT

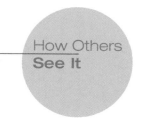
Bartimaeus was determined to get Jesus' attention. J. C. Ryle, in his commentary *Expository Thoughts on the Gospels: Luke,* shared how he could not be silenced:

"'He only cried so much the more.' He felt his need, and found words to tell his story. He was not to be stopped by the rebukes of people who knew nothing of the misery of blindness. His sense of wretchedness made him go on crying. And his importunity was amply rewarded. He found what he sought. That very day he received sight."

Bartimaeus knew his need at its deepest level. Ron Ritchie addressed this in his sermon "Do You Have Faith to Begin a New Life":

"'Have mercy on me,' cried the blind man. Mercy is the grace of God extended toward those who are helpless, those who can't change their circumstances. Have you ever felt helpless, that you have no hope, that you are at your wit's end? This is when God hears the prayers of his people. If we have never cried out for mercy, we are not living realistically."

Zooming **In**

The thirteen-mile road between Jericho and Jerusalem is almost as treacherous today as it was in Jesus' day. The road wanders alongside a deep canyon known as Wadi Qilt. If you traveled the route today, you might catch a glimpse of ancient aqueducts, the caves of Byzantine monks, or the beautiful Saint George's Monastery.

Beggars like Bartimaeus were common in Jesus' time. The money designated for the poor was called *alms,* a word derived from a Greek word meaning "mercifulness." Jewish law forbade driving away a beggar without offering him alms. Generally, women who were poor did not beg. Supporting needy women was more acceptable than supporting needy men.

God gets people involved in almost all of what he does. Bartimaeus discovered that. Don't be surprised if God pulls you into his plans.

Isn't it wonderful that God desires a relationship with you? How would you answer his question "What do you wish for me to do?"

_____

_____

_____

_____

Step out from your circumstances toward Jesus and meet him face-to-face. Do you see all of who he is? How might you ask for him to heal you spiritually?

_____

_____

_____

_____

All around you are women who need a friend to encourage them. What are ways you can be more available to what God is doing in their lives?

_____

_____

_____

_____

Shook-Up Faith

Jesus' eleven disciples went to a mountain in Galilee, where Jesus had told them to meet him. They saw him and worshiped him, but some of them doubted. Jesus came to them and said: I have been given all authority in heaven and on earth! Go to the people of all nations and make them my disciples.

Matthew 28:16–19 CEV

The Big Picture

The night before Jesus was arrested and put to death, he shared precious moments and a meal with his disciples. He warned them about all that was about to happen, but then he encouraged them. He told them they would see him again. "After I am raised up, I will meet you in Galilee." They must have been puzzled, but then it happened just as he said.

The next days were a nightmare of confusion and horror. Jesus was killed on the cross. Jesus' followers were filled with grief. But after three days Jesus rose from the dead. The women found him by his tomb. The disciples saw him on the road and in Jerusalem. He was alive. He told them again, "I will meet you in Galilee."

Thomas, one of the disciples, hadn't seen Jesus yet, and he struggled with doubt. Then one day Jesus stood before him. Could it really be him? He wanted to be sure this was the one he had loved and served. Jesus asked him to touch his wounds, and Thomas's doubts melted away.

The word spread to Jesus' followers that he really was alive and would be in Galilee. No one knows how many made the journey—possibly as many as five hundred. They traveled to the mountain in Galilee to see and hear Jesus speak. When he appeared, they began to worship him, but some still doubted. *Is this Jesus? Is he really alive?*

Jesus came nearer and the crowd hushed. He spoke of the authority God the Father had given him. Then he gave them a mission. "I stand behind you in power. So, go now to all the nations. Tell them about me. Not just the Jews, but everyone."

He was calling them to a difficult task—and a dangerous one. He had been killed for doing this very thing. He was asking them to go beyond their comfort zone, and beyond their borders.

"Remember all I have taught you and go teach others to do the same."

He had taught them how to be devoted to God. Yes, they would teach others.

Jesus finished with: "Remember, I am with you always until the end of time."

What challenge, what peace—Jesus stood before them alive, and with power and authority. They had seen him themselves. They believed. Now they would go tell others that he lives. Jesus, the Messiah, the King of kings, lives.

When you turn to God you discover He has been facing you all the time.

Zig Ziglar

On a farm in California is a hill tucked among the pines, surrounded by picturesque barns. In the springtime, more than 300,000 daffodils bloom. Don't believe it? Maybe you have to see things for yourself to believe—like Thomas—like those who went to the mountain in Galilee. Jesus is comfortable with doubt.

The "doubters" went to the mountain with the others because they loved Jesus, but were still uncertain about what had happened. When they first saw him, some still questioned if it really was Jesus. They weren't trying to cause trouble; they simply wanted to know. In fact, so much that they willingly climbed, not a hill, but a mountain to face their questions. That kind of honest searching can never end in disappointment. It leads to truth.

That day on the Galilean mountain, Jesus faced a mixture of worship and doubt. Unfazed by those doubts, he came to them. *Proserchomai,* the Greek for "came," means "to draw near." As he did, their searching led them to the beautiful reality of his resurrection—God would not be held down by death. When the people left that mountain, their doubt had turned to strengthened faith, a faith they would confidently, and willingly, share with others.

> *Faith given back to us after a night of doubt is a stronger thing, and far more valuable to us, than faith that has never been tested.*
>
> Elizabeth Goudge

Whether you're new at getting to know God, or very familiar with his loving presence, doubts are bound to occasionally sneak in. It's okay to be uncertain, to be hesitant, to ask honest questions, and to wonder. In those moments, when your faith trembles, Jesus doesn't disappear. He draws near.

Apply It
to Your Life

Think of your doubt as an opportunity, a gift—like a lavender-scented invitation to journey toward deeper faith. Open it. Take all the questions tumbling around in your heart and allow the search to begin. Go where you can meet the true Jesus—to others who have known God long and well, to places of worship that love and honor his words.

Take the journey and don't stop, no matter how steep the climb. Ask your questions, no matter how difficult they seem. Jesus can survive your honest examination. He always has, and he always will.

And those questions that linger—see those as gifts, too. Let them prod you toward the beauty of believing without seeing, of certainty, birthed in the depths of the heart, that only comes by God's Spirit.

Either way, you'll find what faith in Jesus is all about. Discover him; then discover him some more.

Draw near to God, and He will draw near to you.
James 4:8 HCSB

Albert Barnes, in his commentary *Barnes' Notes on the New Testament,* wrote about the doubts of those who questioned Jesus' resurrection. He said:

"The mention of their doubting shows that they were honest men . . . that they were convinced only by the strength of the evidence. Their caution in examining the evidence; their slowness to believe; their firm conviction after all their doubts; and their willingness to show their conviction, even by their death, is most conclusive proof that they were not deceived in regard to the fact of his resurrection."

Those on the mountain who saw Jesus both worshipped and doubted. In his sermon "Conquest of Love," Scott Grant discussed this unusual mix:

"What does Jesus do in response to this strange combination of worship and doubt? Two things: he approaches them, and he speaks to them. He is not put off by their doubt. He finds nothing in them that makes it necessary for him to keep his distance, not even their doubt. Then he speaks to them; he speaks into their doubt. In our doubt, Jesus doesn't back away from us. On the contrary, he moves toward us."

Zooming **In**

One of the mountains where Jesus might have met his followers is Mount Hermon. It is northeast of the Sea of Galilee and part of the Anti-Lebanon mountain range. Its highest peak of 9,230 feet is outside of Israel's borders today, but Mizpe Shelagim, a snow observatory at 7,295 feet, is within Israel. One of the psalms speaks of an abundance of water on this mountain. It's true. The mountain receives an average of sixty inches of precipitation a year. Because of its abundance of snow, the Arabs call the mountain *Jabel A-talg,* which means "the snow mountain." Spring runoff feeds the Jordan River.

take a CLOSER look for women

Those who doubted went to the mountain in Galilee to find the truth. They found Jesus. Go toward Jesus with your uncertainties, and let him draw near.

Through the
Eyes of
Your Heart

Don't feel ashamed regarding your doubts about God. Bring them out into the open. Think of a friend who knows God well who might help you. What would you tell her?

_____

_____

_____

In those moments of uncertainty, have you felt that God is far away? Do you see now that he is near? How might you draw close to him even with your doubts?

_____

_____

_____

Certainty can come simply by God's Spirit telling you that something is so. Are you comfortable with that kind of journey too? What kind of relationship with him does that take?

_____

_____

_____

_____

Surely Not I

> The LORD turned to him and said, "Go with the strength you have and rescue Israel from the Midianites. I am sending you!" "But Lord," Gideon replied, "how can I rescue Israel? My clan is the weakest in the whole tribe of Manasseh, and I am the least in my entire family!" The LORD said to him, "I will be with you."
>
> Judges 6:14–16 NLT

The Big Picture

Fear freezes. It causes you to forget that you have a powerful God whose strength can help you. The Israelites let that fear drive them into a horrible existence.

Like wayward children who forget their parents' guidance, Israel often disobeyed. This time they wandered right into the oppressive clutches of the Midianites—a nation so frightening that the Israelites hid, making their homes in caves.

In the springtime, the people ventured out of their holes to plant crops, but the Midianites and neighboring nations attacked again. For seven years the enemy swarmed and destroyed everything in their path. The Israelites feared they might not survive. They finally asked God for help.

God loved Israel and planned to deliver them. He appeared as an angel by an oak in the town of Ophrah. Nearby, a man named Gideon was secretly threshing wheat inside a wine vat. Wheat was usually threshed at the top of the hill so the wind could blow the chaff away, but Gideon was afraid he'd be discovered and killed.

God overlooked Gideon's cowardice. "God is with you, valiant warrior."

Gideon believed he was talking to a messenger of God. "If God is with us, why are the Midianites crushing us? God brought us out of Egypt, but now he has abandoned us."

"Go in the strength you have. I am sending you to rescue Israel."

"Not me. I am as inadequate as they come. My family is the least powerful of our tribe, and I'm the weakest of my family."

"I will be with you," said God, "and you will get rid of the Midianites as if you were dealing with one man."

Would he? Over the next days, Gideon sought assurance that he had heard God correctly. He asked for signs. Would an animal fleece, set out all night, remain dry when the morning dew came? How about if in the morning the fleece was wet, but there had been no morning dew? God patiently provided the signs and assured Gideon.

Then he sent Gideon to battle. Would Gideon now trust him? No matter what? He directed Gideon to drop the numbers of his army from 22,000 to 10,000, then all the way to 300. This small army would defeat the ruthless Midianites with only trumpets and torches. The seemingly impossible victory convinced the Israelites *and* Gideon that God truly was with them.

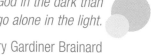

I would rather walk with God in the dark than go alone in the light.

Mary Gardiner Brainard

You may have avoided a potential confrontation with someone by pushing your shopping cart down a different isle. Gideon chose a winepress. Out of all the warriors God could have chosen to deliver Israel, he chose a fearful man. Notice what God told Gideon: "Go in the strength you have."

"What strength?" Gideon responded as he hid in a winepress. He felt he was the last person to help defeat the Midianites and free Israel. God saw it differently. He called him a valiant warrior, perhaps partly because Gideon's name means a "hacker" or "one who hewed down." But even more, God saw the potential in Gideon. *Valor* is *chayil* in Hebrew. It refers to force, strength, and virtue. Gideon may not have been very brave at the time, but God saw a quality character.

As Gideon got to know God better, he found God's mighty strength behind his own small measure of strength. He heard God tell him, "I am sending you," and "I will be with you." Gideon's strength alone could not defeat Israel's enemies, but with God's power, presence, and direction, the nation would know victory. Gideon discovered the greatest strength he had was that which he found in God.

> *God does not require us to have arrived, only to be moving in the right direction.*
>
> Sarah Horsman

Some mornings you wake up and find yourself uneasy about what your day holds. You might feel stretched to the point of breaking and wonder how you're going to make it through. When that happens, it's tempting to pull the covers over your head and nestle back into a soft pillow. Since you probably don't have that luxury, you're going to have to do something different.

Before you pull yourself away from the comfort of your bed, take time to invite God into your day and into those moments ahead that you most fear. Tell him that you desire to hear his voice over the thunderous beating of your anxious heart. And then listen. He'll assure you as he assured Gideon.

"I will be with you."

He will be. Remember that as you swing your feet out of your bed and step out of your nightgown. When you join the others in your home or go out your front door, run those words through your mind. Trust them. Trust who said them. Then, in those moments during your day when you feel hesitant, remember, the strength you have is enough when God is with you.

He gives power to the faint, and to him who has no might he increases strength.

Isaiah 40:29 ESV

How Others See It

In *Judges (Believers Church Bible Commentary)*, T. L. Brensinger pointed out God's response to Gideon's lingering doubts and fears:

"Rather than insisting that Gideon immediately rise to the desired level of commitment, the Lord nurtures him through his moments of weakness. While not condoning evasiveness or prolonged excuse-making, God deals graciously and patiently with all of the Gideons of the world who genuinely need help and reassurance."

Gideon became known as a hero. J. Sidlow Baxter, in *Explore the Book,* highlights the source of his valor:

"Gideon, the fifth judge of Israel, is rightly counted as one of the outstanding heroes in Israel's early history. Yet we need to realize at the outset that his heroism was not a product of his natural make-up, but the outcome of a transforming spiritual experience. It is this which gives him a living significance to ourselves today."

Zooming **In**

Ancient winepresses were dug out of solid rock or earth at the depth of two or three feet. Earth presses were lined with stonework and pitch. One vat would lie above and next to another. Juice from the crushed grapes flowed from the upper vat down a channel into the lower vat. Many of these winepresses still exist today.

Syria and Palestine have an abundance of natural and man-made caves carved out of their limestone, sandstone, and chalk hills and mountains. Many of the caves in these regions are massive in size. One complex of caves still visible near Damascus in Syria can hold four thousand men.

Gideon's lack of courage didn't stop God from involving him in a bold plan, and it won't stop him from involving you. When he does, be assured that he will be with you, too.

Through the
Eyes of
Your Heart

In fear, Gideon hid in a winepress where he couldn't do his job well. What causes you to hide in fear? What does your fear prevent you from doing well?

_____

_____

_____

_____

God saw Gideon differently than Gideon saw himself. You are God's child, a woman of potential and worth. Is that what you see when you look in the mirror?

_____

_____

_____

_____

"Go in the strength you have," is a challenge to move forward regardless of your fears. Write a prayer of triumph over your fears.

_____

_____

_____

_____

Joyfully Expectant

They were excited, and everyone ran to see them at the place called Solomon's Porch. The man wouldn't let go of Peter and John. When Peter saw this, he said to the people, "Men of Israel, why are you amazed about this man? Why are you staring at us as though we have made him walk by our own power or godly life?"

Acts 3:11–12 GOD'S WORD

The Big Picture

It was at the gate called Beautiful: the perfect spot, on a perfect afternoon, for a gracious miracle. The streets were bustling with the usual crowds who were entering the city and visiting the temple. A lame man gazed at the eyes of those passing. He looked for signs of compassion. For all of his adult life he had faced this humiliation—carried like a child to the streets to beg.

The more profitable times of the day were when the Jews visited the temple court for prayer—at nine, noon, and three. During these hours the lame man worked hard. His livelihood depended on it.

"Please, could you help a lame man?" he called out to those who walked nearby.

Two stopped in front of him, and he looked their way hopefully. One of them said, "I don't have any money for you, but what I have I gladly give."

He'd give what he had? Food or clothing? Perhaps a coat?

"In the name of Jesus Christ of Nazareth, get up. Walk!"

What was this man talking about? He couldn't —

Next thing he knew one of the men bent down, grabbed hold of his hands, and helped him stand. Suddenly his legs were steady and holding him up. His ankles and feet were straight. God had healed him. The joy of it coursed through his body. He could walk, run, and leap—and he did. He clung to the two men as they continued into the temple court. "Praise God," he shouted. "Praise God."

Everyone rushed to see what the commotion was. He could hear their exclamations and questions: The lame man, who sat every day at the Beautiful Gate, is walking. How could this be? And who are those men he's holding on to? Isn't that Peter and John, Jesus' disciples? Did they perform this miracle?

The man named Peter saw their amazement and began to speak: "People, why are you surprised to see this man walk? You're acting as though we did it. Do you think we have power to accomplish this? Do you think our devout lives brought this about?"

They were a typical crowd, curious, and caught up in the excitement of the healing that had occurred. Peter felt they were slipping into viewing him and John as holy, and having divine power of their own. He quickly corrected their misconceptions. God had performed this beautiful healing. Only he had that power.

God's gifts put man's best dreams to shame.

Elizabeth Barrett Browning

Miracle wrinkle-remover, miracle diets, miracle cures. "Miracle" anything stirs up excitement. The lame man's miracle was real, and it stirred up a whole crowd. Peter took the opportunity to direct their attention in the proper direction—toward God. Notice the man wouldn't let go of Peter and John. Even he needed to be reminded to cling to God instead.

The healed man praised God, but still clung to the men. The Greek word *krateo* used here means "to use strength to seize, hold fast to, and retain." He didn't want to let go. The full strength of his feet and legs had returned; he didn't need the men for balance. Perhaps his gratefulness for them overwhelmed him, and he didn't want them to leave. Or maybe he feared letting go might bring the return of his lame condition. Either way, Peter's question was appropriate: why look to us, mere men, as if we had the power and holiness to heal?

It's natural to look first to the instrument of the miracle before the source. Peter pointed toward the source: Look at God. It is he who heals and whom you should seize hold of and retain in your grasp. In your wonder, gratefulness, and love, cling to him.

> *Miracles are a retelling in small letters of the very same story which is written across the whole world in letters too large for some of us to see.*
>
> C. S. Lewis

The lame man didn't expect a miracle that day as he sat by the gate called Beautiful. It was another day of the usual, his lot in life.

Consider what you've grown to accept as your lot in life. Like the lame man, you may fully believe your situation will never change. Every day you face the routine, its challenges and disappointments. It's not fun, but for you, it's reality. It could have become so familiar that you have a *krateo*-like grip on it. If you want to be joyfully expectant to receive all that God has for you, you will need to let go, to hope, to believe, and to ask.

Where God begins the change, sometimes, is not in the circumstances, but in your perception of the circumstances. Maybe you can't see the full picture yet—all the colors of the painting of you becoming the woman he intends for you to become. Sometimes catching the vision is all it takes. Let go of the dreary daily resignation, and begin to live fully and expectantly in all that God has for you. Seize it as if you never want to let go. Seize him.

You will make known to me the path of life; in Your presence is fullness of joy; in Your right hand there are pleasures forever.

Psalm 16:11 NASB

What happened to the lame man was clearly God's work. In *The Book of Acts* in The New International Commentary on the New Testament series, F. F. Bruce said:

"There was no merely magical efficacy in the sounds which Peter pronounced when he commanded the cripple to walk in Jesus' name; the cripple would have known no benefit had he not responded in faith in what Peter said; but once this response was made, the power of the risen Christ filled his body with health and strength."

In *Acts* in The Tyndale New Testament Commentaries series, I. Howard Marshall noted how Peter used the natural curiosity of the onlookers to share about God:

"Peter seizes on the way in which the crowds were quite naturally gazing at John and himself as the possessors of the remarkable power which had healed the man. They would have regarded them either as being possessed of remarkable powers of their own or as being so devout that God would respond to their prayers with miraculous signs. . . . Peter wanted to direct their attention away from the apostles to the source of the miracle."

Zooming **In**

During the first century, Jerusalem's temple and surrounding courts sat on the east side of the city overlooking the Kidron Valley. If people entered the old city from the east, they would come through the Golden Gate, the closest outside gate to where the temple stood. Inside the city walls is the site of the Gate Beautiful. People walked from the Court of Gentiles through this gate into a place of public worship. Both gates are cited as a possible place for the healing of the lame man, but the latter is more likely. The Golden Gate is the oldest of the gates, but it has remained walled up for twelve centuries.

What beauty your eyes will see as you learn to watch for the miracles in each day. What delight you will experience as you expect God to surprise you with them.

Each day is filled with miracles—gifts from God. Do you see them? Describe the miracles you saw in yesterday, the potential ones in today.

_____

_____

_____

_____

What have you grown used to in your life? If you were to paint a different picture, what would it look like? How might you become joyfully expectant to see it happen?

_____

_____

_____

One miracle you have in each day is your relationship with God. What can you plan to do to hold fast to him, to seize him and all that he has for you right now?

_____

_____

_____

_____

The Wonder Before You

"Our whole being is dried up; there is nothing at all except this manna before our eyes!" Now the manna was like coriander seed, and its color like the color of bdellium.

Numbers 11:6–7 NKJV

The Big Picture

Discontentment tends to set root, then grow until nothing you believe has any basis in reality. This was all too true for the Hebrews God rescued out of Egypt.

Through one miracle after another, God helped the Israelites—two million of them—escape a tyrannical pharaoh and his ruthless army. With Moses as their guide, they were led to safety into the wilderness of the Sinai Peninsula. They were on their way to a new land, a place of promise and freedom. In their travels across the desert, God protected them day and night and provided all they needed. The people were thankful for a while, then the grumbling began—and seemed to never end.

Wasn't it just a short trip to Canaan? Why are we still in the desert? Why did Moses take us out of Egypt? We want to go back.

The Israelites were like fussy children on a long trip, but God, like an ever-patient parent, continued to love them.

One way he helped them was to provide an unusual, nutritious food they

take a CLOSER look for women

named manna, meaning "what is it?" For this miraculous food, God provided specific instructions: Six days a week the manna would appear like frost on the ground, after the morning dew. The people would gather only what they needed—an *omer,* or two quarts, for each person. On the sixth day, they could collect double portions so they had enough for the seventh day, a day to rest. The only time it could be kept over, and not spoil, was for this last day of the week.

The manna was a remarkable food, with the appearance of tiny coriander seeds and the color of a precious, coveted resin called bdellium. The Israelites boiled the manna and made porridge, or shaped it into delicious cakes.

But the people couldn't break their habit of discontentment. It wasn't long before they grew tired of God's gift. "Oh, how we wish we had the food we had in Egypt—the fish and the melons, the cucumbers, garlic, and leeks," they grumbled. "We are wasting away, for we have nothing at all but manna."

As is usually true of discontentment, the Israelites had lost sight of all the good they had. They were no longer thankful for anything God had provided. Their perspective made for a miserable trip for all.

I have kept my soul calm and quiet. My soul is content as a weaned child is content in its mother's arms.

Psalm 131:2 GOD'S WORD

The Israelites had become blind to the fullness of what God had provided. Notice the stark contrast between the beauty and uniqueness of the manna, and their perception of it. In their discontentment, the Israelites had created their own reality. How easy it is to do that—to entirely miss seeing the beauty in front of you, even in the mirror, and wish for something else.

It must have been amazing the morning the manna first appeared—like waking up to a fresh snow, or discovering the enchanting first buds of spring. You can imagine the excitement that rippled through the camp. "Look, it's small and fragrant like coriander seed." "Yes, and it has the iridescence of bdellium." "Taste it, it's delicious." "What a precious gift from God."

Unfortunately, that didn't last long.

Discontentment has shaky scaffolding. It's usually created from a made-up reality. That was true for the Israelites as well. They hadn't been comfortable in Egypt. They were slaves. They surely didn't have the abundance of food they described, not under a pharaoh who did what he could to destroy them.

When they began to grumble, nothing had changed in the sufficiency or goodness of what God had given. So what was reality? God, and what he provides, is always sufficient, always enough. Always.

> Contentment is a pearl of great price, and whoever procures it at the expense of ten thousand desires makes a wise and happy purchase.
>
> John Balguy

Each day offers a delightful opportunity for you to discover the "manna" God has brought to you—the wonders and sufficiency of even the smallest provision. Do you see it?

Two women could have exactly the same things in life, yet one could be happy while the other is miserable. Why? It's all about attitude.

One sees all she has and is thankful to God for each gift. When she notices any lack, she trusts that God knows, and will provide at the right time. Her focus stays on the good. She enjoys the fragrance of a single rose without yearning for a rose garden.

The other finds this difficult to do, but what can she do? She can take time to remember her first moments of delight in the gifts and wonders God has given. She can begin to believe again that he knows her every need. In each day, she can watch for the single rose that will fill her heart with joy.

What has God brought into your day? What is the "manna" he has provided to encourage you and remind you that he loves you and cares for you? It's here. What is it?

When You give it to them, they gather it; when You open Your hand, they are satisfied with good things.

Psalm 104:28 HCSB

How Others
See It

God provided manna in the morning that fed the Israelites all day. Taking time for morning prayers can be spiritual manna for you. Andrew Murray in his book *Abide in Christ* discussed this:

"The morning manna fed all the day; it is only when the believer in the morning secures his quiet time in secret to renew distinctly and effectually loving fellowship with his Savior that the abiding can be kept up all the day. . . . In the morning, with its freshness and quiet, the believer can look out upon the day. . . . Christ is his manna, his nourishment, his strength, his life: he can take the day's portion for the day, Christ as his for all the needs the day may bring, and go on in the assurance that the day will be one of blessing and of growth."

Zooming **In**

From 1972 to 1982 an Israeli university surveyed an area of northern Sinai. Archaeologists discovered pottery shards and other evidences of ancient occupation in 284 sites. It looked as if many people were wandering across the desert. Some sites seemed to be base camps, but there was no evidence of buildings. The people most likely lived in booths, tents, or lean-tos.

Bdellium, to which the Hebrews compared manna, is an aromatic gum resin that comes from a tree similar to a balsam. Today it is found most often in India and Arabia. A sixteenth-century herbalist named Parkinson noted that when you cut the bark of the tree, the gum oozed out and formed fragrant, bead-like pearls.

When circumstances or relationships are difficult, it's easy to think back to another time when you thought you were happier. Ask God to help you remember the preciousness of what you presently have.

Where are you struggling with contentment? Consider all the beauty and wonder you once saw. Is there something you can capture again?

_____

_____

_____

Frustrations can make things look fuzzy. Look honestly for what is real in that fuzziness. What do you see? What needs to be brought into clearer focus again?

_____

_____

_____

_____

God's provision is always sufficient. Ask him to help you find the simple joys in your day and see them as treasures. What comes to mind right now?

_____

_____

_____

_____

It's Too Heavy

Since we are surrounded by so great a cloud of witnesses, let us also lay aside every weight, and sin which clings so closely, and let us run with endurance the race that is set before us, looking to Jesus, the founder and perfecter of our faith.

Hebrews 12:1–2 ESV

The Big Picture

Choosing to be a follower of Christ in the first century wasn't easy. Dedicated believers faced harassment and insults from the Jewish leaders and Roman officials. Many were falsely accused, lost all they owned, or were sent into hiding. Others were chased down and beaten, imprisoned, or killed.

It was during this time that the letter to the Hebrews was written. The unknown author spoke specifically to the Hebrew Christians—those who struggled with remaining faithful in their commitment to Christianity. Some desired to return to the familiar Jewish sacrificial system instead of maintaining their belief that Christ was the final sacrifice. Blending back into the Jewish culture seemed appealing. They had grown weary of persecution.

"Remember," is what the writer told his readers. "Think back to the early days when you first learned about Jesus. You endured hard struggles, yet you remained faithful."

Picture the readers holding the tattered letter that had passed through many hands. As they read the list of the sufferings they had endured, they nodded their heads in acknowledgment.

take a CLOSER look for women

Remember.

"You helped the prisoners, and even joyfully accepted the consequences when your possessions were taken away. You knew of a better, long-lasting possession—God's love for you through Jesus. Don't let go of your confidence. Endure. You will be glad you did. Jesus will come back for you. Live in faith."

And then the readers pored over the next words, those that recounted the history of the many faithful ones who had gone before them. "Believe in the faithfulness of God," the writer challenged. "He rewards those who continually seek him. Look at Noah who trusted God's warning and built a boat to save his family; Abraham who left everything familiar and traveled far away to a land God showed him; Sarah, who, though past childbearing age, believed God's promise of a child and a nation; Rahab, who helped the spies and knew God would protect her when her city was destroyed—these and others who remained steadfast in their trust of God."

Remember.

"Think about these faithful ones who believed God through long-awaited promises, unknown paths, and difficult trials. They are your audience, cheering you on in your pursuit of victory. Remove anything that slows you down from obtaining that victory. Run hard toward Jesus."

Remember. Endure. You can do it.

There are certain weights in life you simply cannot carry. Your Lord is asking you to set them down and trust Him. What do you say we take God up on His offer?

Max Lucado

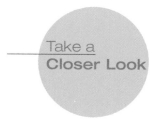

Imagine trying to run a race—especially one fraught with obstacles—while lugging a trunk full of family memorabilia—old family albums, cookbooks, and gowns. That's almost what the Hebrew people were trying to do. The writer of the letter compared living the Christian life to running a race, but the "weights" they carried were putting their race in jeopardy.

The Hebrew letter revealed what those weights were. The people had become overwhelmed with the challenges of living a Christian life amid the first-century persecutions. Their passion was waning, and they were tempted to return to old traditions. The Greek word for *weights* is *ogkos*. It means "burden" or "impediment," but it also means "a bulging mass" or "tumor."

Like tumors that enlarge and destroy, the Hebrews' worries and distractions threatened to not only slow down, but even bring death to the progress of their Christian faith. The writer gave his readers a solution: Strip away every destructive way of thinking as you would unneeded, heavy clothing. Get rid of anything that hinders your growing faith. Then lift your head and focus on Jesus. You began this race for him. He will help you complete it.

> *Courage can't see around corners, but goes around them anyway.*
>
> Mignon McLaughlin

It can be difficult to passionately pursue God every day, but in light of the Hebrew writer's challenge, what an opportunity you have. You have an exciting run ahead, but it will be much richer if you get rid of the "weights" you're carrying.

Apply It
to Your Life

Look at your weights. They can be different for each woman, but anything that distracts you from deepening your spiritual life with Jesus is a weight. They can hinder and slow you down. They can consume your time and energy, and crowd out intimate moments with God. They can keep you from clearly seeing him standing at your finish line.

If you're like most, you have a lot of weights. That's okay. Set goals and deal with them one at a time. Check to see if some of your weights need to be shed entirely from your life, or if you only need a time adjustment. Give a friend a call, and ask her to be your accountability partner. She, along with others, can be your "crowd of witnesses" cheering you on.

Now run hard. Run with every ounce of faith you have in Jesus, and in what he's doing in you. Run free of your weights, and don't look back. Make it a great race. Finish well.

Athletes exercise self-control in all things; they do it to receive a perishable wreath, but we an imperishable one.

1 Corinthians 9:25 NRSV

The Hebrew writer mentioned two encumbrances to running a good spiritual race. F. B. Meyer, in *The Way into the Holiest: Exposition of the Epistle to the Hebrews,* clarified the difference between "sin" with "weights":

"A sin is that which in its very nature, and always, and by whomsoever perpetrated, is a transgression of God's law, a violation of God's will. But a weight is something which in itself, or to another, may be harmless, or even legitimate, but in our own case is a hindrance and an impediment."

In the same work, F. B. Meyer talked about the types of weights people might carry around today:

"All such things may be considered as weights. It may be a friendship which is too engrossing; a habit which is sapping away our energy as the taproot the fruit bearing powers of a tree; a pursuit, an amusement, a pastime, a system of reading, a method of spending time, too fascinating and too absorbing, and therefore harmful to the soul—which is tempted to walk when it should run, and to loiter when it should haste."

Zooming **In**

Athleticism is very much a part of Hebrew history and culture. Jacob rolled away a stone from a well, and David fought off a lion and a bear to save his father's sheep. Early weight lifting consisted of lifting and holding heavy stones above the head. Archery, javelin throwing, and juggling were recreational sports, as were swimming and running. In 7 BC, Herod the Great introduced the Olympic games in Jerusalem by erecting a sports theater in honor of Caesar. Many Jews feared these games would corrupt the Jewish way of life with their pagan focus. Some rabbis, however, respected athletics as part of Greek wisdom, and encouraged gymnastics among the youth.

The Hebrew people were encouraged to run unburdened and free toward all God had for them. You also have a race to run—a life race. Run it well.

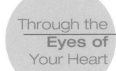 Consider the value of what you are running toward. Until you see that goal clearly, your run won't matter. What do you want your life to be about? How is God a part of that?

_____

_____

_____

The Hebrews looked back to what they used to have instead of what they had in Jesus. What old habits, routines, or traditions have become weights for you? How will you let them go?

_____

_____

_____

A race without those who cheer you on is much too lonely. Think of several women you can ask to be your encouragers. In what ways can you help one another run your life race well?

_____

_____

_____

_____

Comfortable Limitations

Moses said to the LORD, "O Lord, I have never been eloquent, neither in the past nor since you have spoken to your servant. I am slow of speech and tongue." The LORD said to him, "Who gave man his mouth? Who makes him deaf or mute? Who gives him sight or makes him blind? Is it not I, the LORD?"

Exodus 4:10–11 NIV

The Big Picture

Moses only thought he was going to live a quiet life as a shepherd. God had different plans.

As a young man, Moses witnessed Egypt's cruelty toward the Israelites. Though he had grown up in the pharaoh's house, he opposed the slavery of his people, so much so that the pharaoh sought to kill him. He fled to the land of Midian where he started a family and became a shepherd. Many years later, the pharaoh who sought Moses' life died.

Egypt's new pharaoh was as stubborn and cruel as the one before. He refused to free the Israelites from their lives as slaves, and they began to lose hope of a different life. God was ready to bring Moses back into the picture.

It was now forty years into Moses' quiet life in the Midian wilderness. Things were about to drastically change. God paid Moses a visit—and what a way to present himself. He supernaturally appeared in a bush blazing with fire but, amazingly, not burning up.

"Moses," God called.

take a CLOSER look for women

Moses approached the bush and realized it was God. At God's request, he removed his shoes, and then he answered, "I am here."

God explained Israel's situation in Egypt. He then told Moses, "I'm sending you to lead the people out of Egypt."

"Me? Who am I to go?"

God assured Moses that he would be with him.

"What could I say that would help?"

God provided directions, including exactly what Moses would say to the Israelite elders and how he was to go before the pharaoh.

Moses then began a whole string of what-ifs. "What if they won't believe that you sent me? What if they don't do what I ask?" God answered each with further instructions and assurances. With God's help, the Israelites would believe him. Moses still wasn't convinced he should go. "Please, God, I don't speak well, and I never will. My speech is slow and faltering."

"Who made everyone's mouth? Who gives the ability to speak or not speak, to see or not see? I do. Now go, Moses. I will help you speak and teach you what to say."

Moses continued to beg God to send someone else. Though God consented to send his brother Aaron with him, he still planned to accomplish the rescue through Moses—in spite of Moses' lack of confidence and ability.

A healthy self-image is being committed to the truth of God's estimation of you.

Josh McDowell

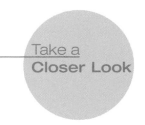
Moses groaned and complained. He didn't feel he had the ability to do what God asked of him. Notice God himself said it is *he* who makes each person able or not able to see, hear, or speak. God made Moses the way he was, and he was made just right—like you.

The Hebrew word for *made* in this verse is *siym.* It means "to appoint" or "put in place." God establishes the order of things, including the intricacies of the eyes, ears, and mouth, and how they function . . . or, as this verse says, don't function.

Moses felt insecure with what he saw as his weaknesses. In his perception, these could only hinder what God wanted to accomplish. But God didn't see it that way; he could work powerfully through Moses in ways he never would imagine. Moses only needed to trust him.

Think of it—to be chosen as an instrument of God to change history, and to experience God's power working through you. What an opportunity. What a gift. Something you may not even notice if it weren't for your weaknesses.

> *True humility is not an abject, groveling, self-despising spirit; it is but a right estimate of ourselves as God sees us.*
>
> Tryon Edwards

Flowers grow in the garden, unique and beautiful—just as God planned. None are perfect, but who defines a flaw?

In spite of anything you may view as a weakness or disability, you have an opportunity for God to use you every single day.

Like the flowers in the garden, you are made unique. But you see flaws? Who told you they were flaws? These "weaknesses" are simply a part of how God created you and how he can best love you, and love through you. You can be an instrument of his extraordinary work—a work that can only be accomplished through your unique set of characteristics and circumstances.

In those moments when you are discouraged by what you feel you can't do well—for *any* reason—see this as an opportunity to learn to trust God a little more. You are his daughter, special in his eyes. He made you just the way you are, and he sees you as perfectly suited to do a most amazing work. He will be with you and teach you how.

Go forward, confident of what God will accomplish through all that you are. Live each day in expectation of the miracles ahead.

He said to me, "My grace is enough for you. When you are weak, my power is made perfect in you."

2 Corinthians 12:9 NCV

Moses struggled with his weaknesses, but as John Piper pointed out, he knew God could intervene. In his sermon "Who Made Man's Mouth," he said:

"Moses' assumption was, God should only pick people with special natural abilities to deliver his word. But there are several flaws in that assumption, and Moses is aware of at least one of them. We can see it in verse 10. Moses knows that God can take a person with no eloquence and then give it to him, changing him into an eloquent, persuasive speaker."

Scott Grant, in his sermon "Divinely Deficient," explained why he felt God allowed weaknesses:

"He says he is responsible for them! . . . Why? . . . Because what we really need is faith. God loves us too much to give us something we don't need. What we need is faith, and that's what he wants to give. The Lord says to Moses, 'Now then go, and I, even I, will be with your mouth and teach you what you are to say.'"

Zooming **In**

Moses removed his sandals before God. Then and today, taking off your shoes is a sign of respect in the Middle East. Shoes are removed in holy places because the sole of a shoe, worn on the lowest part of the body, is always in contact with unclean things. In India, "Jooté maro!" or "Hit him with your shoes!" is considered a demeaning remark.

The word *disability* doesn't appear in the Bible, but some in Moses' time were blind, deaf, lame, or dealt with disease and deformities. Many Hebrews connected physical wellness with virtue and even forbade those with physical challenges from serving in the priesthood. Jesus later made it clear that it was the heart attitude that mattered.

Weaknesses can be seen as strengths; they allow you to trust God to do something through you that you wouldn't try otherwise.

Moses was exactly suited for what God had in mind for Israel, and you are beautifully suited for God's design for your life. How can you begin to change your perspective of yourself?

_____

_____

_____

Everyone has things they don't do very well, or do at all. How might those very things launch you into a new adventure with God? Describe the possibilities.

_____

_____

_____

_____

What can you try this week that you've never thought you could do? How might what you see as a weakness actually help you rather than hinder you?

_____

_____

_____

_____

Too Much Serving

She had a sister called Mary, who sat at the Lord's feet and listened to his teaching. But Martha was distracted with much serving. And she went up to him and said, "Lord, do you not care that my sister has left me to serve alone? Tell her then to help me."

Luke 10:39–40 ESV

The Big Picture

Martha watched Jesus walking up the road. He must have been weary having traveled all the way from Galilee. He'd planned to stay in Bethany before going on to Jerusalem. She hoped he would stay in her home.

She thought of how Jesus worked tirelessly to teach and serve others. What a powerful man he was, and yet more than a man. It was difficult to grasp, but yes, he was the Messiah, too. And here he was visiting Bethany as their friend.

"Welcome, Jesus," Martha called out. "Please stay with us and make yourself at home." She had heard that Jesus often slept outside with nothing but a rock for a pillow. He'd have much better tonight—a clean, comfortable place to rest, and a good meal.

Jesus came into Martha's home, which she shared with her siblings, Mary and Lazarus. Conversation abounded as they talked of Jesus' ministry and travels, and the disciples. While he talked, Martha bustled through the house.

Get the dishes out . . . get water from the well . . . check the meat . . . make up the beds. . . . She loved Jesus. It was an honor to serve him.

Jesus began to talk about deeper spiritual matters. What was he saying? It was hard to hear with all the details that needed her attention. And where did Mary go? She was helping but now . . . she was sitting down? What did she think she was doing? She should be helping. After stewing a bit, Martha finally brought the matter to Jesus' attention.

"Jesus, aren't you concerned Mary left me to do all the work? Tell her to come help me."

Jesus looked at her tenderly. "Martha, Martha," he began.

So he understood. Soon Mary would be helping again. Good. There was still much to do. But Martha was surprised by what Jesus said next.

"You are stirred up about many things," he said. "Only one thing is important, and Mary has chosen it. I would not want to send her away to do anything different."

Martha looked at her sister sitting there at Jesus' feet. Mary had stopped what she was doing to learn from Jesus. Yes, their special guest was probably hungry and tired, but spending this time with him truly was more important.

Guide me in Your truth and teach me, for You are the God of my salvation; I wait for You all day long.

Psalm 25:5 HCSB

Martha believed her generous hospitality expressed her love for Jesus. Look closely. It wasn't wrong for Martha to use her abilities and interests to serve Jesus, but it was "too much."

Much used in this passage is *polus,* an adverb expressing intensity. You can picture industrious Martha fussing to make everything perfect: prepare the hardiest dishes, set a beautiful table, and certainly keep everything tidy. Martha's preparations for a meal, and taking care of Jesus, were far beyond what he needed. Jesus didn't need "much."

In fact, Martha's busyness distracted her from truly honoring or enjoying her special guest. The Greek word for *distract* is *perispao,* and means "to drag around, to be encumbered with cares and responsibilities." Martha was beautifully gifted, but this couldn't have been pleasant even for someone who enjoyed hospitality.

But it wasn't that Martha should abandon the abilities God gave her; she only needed to consider how and when to best use them. In fact, another time Mary could benefit from Martha's example. At that moment, though, Jesus was there. She could set aside the "much serving" and enjoy that precious time with him.

> *I have held many things in my hands, and have lost them all; but whatever I have placed in God's hands, that I still possess.*
>
> Martin Luther

God created you with amazing uniqueness. You know what you do well, but like Martha, taking it to excess can become "too much." Celebrate the abilities and personality God gave you. Use them to serve others and God . . . in balance.

Apply It
to Your Life

Humor might be in order here. Think about those exaggerated caricatures that county fair cartoonists draw. For a moment consider your "too-much-ness" in that light. Imagine organization, leadership, generosity, thoughtfulness, and any creative ability taken to a humorous extreme. Now look a little closer. Does any part of what you imagined cause you to say, "That kind of looks like me"?

It's okay. See this as an opportunity to adjust either the timing or the intensity of what you do. Bring it down from any level of franticness to a pace that is enjoyable for everyone, including you. And, most important, look for ways to relax and spend time getting to know God better.

Celebrate and thank God for the way he made you. Serve him, and others, with grace and balance.

I will praise You, because I have been remarkably and wonderfully made. Your works are wonderful, and I know [this] very well.

Psalm 139:14 HCSB

Ray Pritchard considered both Martha and Mary loyal followers of Jesus. In his sermon "The Harried Homemaker: Christ Speaks to the Problem of Compulsive Busyness," he said this about Martha:

"Regardless of what else we may think, it is clear that she loves the Lord and does what she does out of love and not obligation. She respects Jesus so much that without hesitation she wants to honor him by using her gifts to prepare a meal in his honor. Her motives are pure even if her attitude is not quite right."

John Calvin believed that Martha's hospitality was commendable but that Jesus desired she not work so hard. In *Matthew, Mark, and Luke* in his New Testament Commentaries, volume 2, Calvin said:

"Martha carried her activity beyond proper bounds; for Christ would rather have chosen to be entertained in a frugal manner, and at moderate expense, than that the holy woman should have submitted to so much toil. . . . Martha, by distracting her attention, and undertaking more labor than was necessary, deprived herself of the advantage of Christ's visit."

Zooming **In**

In Jesus' time, people would enter their homes through courts, or directly by a porch. The rooms inside were furnished with tables, couches, chairs, candlesticks, and lamps. Cushions, ornaments, and pictures were considered luxury items. The roomy dining area was the hub of the home and sometimes used for meetings.

The town of Bethany, where Martha lived, sat just two miles southeast of Jerusalem. Modern-day Bethany is called el-Azariyeh, an Arabic name derived from "Lazarus," the name of Martha's brother. Today the city is part of the West Bank and under Israeli administration. The ruins of the old city still exist, and include several walls of what is believed to be Martha's home.

"Martha, Martha." That might be a good line to say to yourself, with a smile, when you find you are going a little overboard with your talents.

Even when it's helpful, "too much" can be stressful and exhausting. Have you felt that at times? What can you do differently to enjoy what you do well?

_____

_____

_____

_____

Good things can easily become distractions from spending quiet moments with God. How might taking that time to stop help you use your gifts more wisely?

_____

_____

_____

_____

What can you discover from the "Marys" in your life who know how to slow down and enjoy God? How might you encourage each other?

_____

_____

_____

_____

The Promise

The Big Picture

A gift received, and then let go into the hands of God, has great promise.

Hannah wanted to be hungry for the meat her husband, Elkanah, had lovingly given her. It was the best portion of their celebration feast, but she could not eat. They had come from their town of Ramah, up to the high mountains of Shiloh, to attend a festival, and to thank God for the blessings of that year. These annual treks were quickly spoiled by the taunts of Elkanah's other wife, Peninnah. She never failed to gloat over how many children she had, and cruelly reminded Hannah that she would never have any. Hannah began to weep.

"Why are you sad and not eating?" Elkanah asked. "Isn't my love for you better than having many sons?"

Yes, she deeply appreciated his love, but every part of her longed desperately for a child. When everyone finished eating, Hannah drew away to the temple to pray. She wept as she silently pleaded with God. "Please consider

take a CLOSER look for women

your servant's affliction. Think of me and grant me a son. I will give him to you for all of his life," she vowed.

Eli, the priest, saw her lips moving without speaking and approached her. "How long will you keep drinking? Sober up," he told her.

"I am not drunk, only brokenhearted," she explained. "I've been telling God my sorrows. Don't think of me as worthless."

"Go then in peace. May God give you what you have asked for."

The next morning Hannah and Elkanah worshipped God, and then returned to their home. Within the next year, God answered Hannah's prayers, and she bore a son whom she named Samuel. When he grew older, she and Elkanah returned to Shiloh and dedicated their son to God.

"Remember when I prayed for this child?" she told the priest. "God answered. I am now doing what I promised and lending him to God. I give him to you to be trained for service in the tabernacle. He'll belong to God for his entire life." Then Hannah sang a prayer of thanks to God for all to hear. "There is none like you, God," she declared.

A gift was given, a long-awaited son, and Hannah recognized the source of that gift. Samuel grew up to become a prophet and a judge, and he served God his whole life.

With God there is always more unfolding, that what we can glimpse of the divine is always exactly enough, and never enough.

Kathleen Norris

Like a locket close to the heart, Hannah must have cherished baby Samuel, God's answer to her prayer. But instead of keeping the long-awaited gift, she lent him back to God—for his whole life.

To finally be given your heart's desire only to let it go? It seems that would have only caused Hannah further sorrow. What perspective did she have that made giving up this gift possible?

Hannah's vow offers some clues as it shows what she believed about God. Without reservation she trusted that he could, if he chose, grant her request. Then, the best way to thank God would be to dedicate the gift entirely to him. She and Elkanah were from a priestly tribe, the Levites. It was natural for both—like breathing air—to consider the most beautiful and sacred way to live was in the service of God. Samuel would have that kind of life.

Hannah *lent* her son. This word is *shaal* in the Hebrew, and means "lay to charge." She trusted Samuel into God's charge. She wasn't "giving away" her son, but dedicating him into God's trustworthy care. This was cause for celebration, not sorrow; for peace, not anguish.

> *Devout souls delight to look upon those mercies which they have obtained in answer to supplication, for they can see God's special love in them.*
>
> Charles Spurgeon

Hannah's actions strongly reflect the cultural and religious structure of her day, but her example still offers beautiful lessons for today. What would it be like to capture some of Hannah's perspective, to readily see God's gifts when they are given, and long for them to be used in the best possible ways?

Hannah had a daily relationship with God. This helped her more naturally see him as someone she could believe in and trust with everything. God was more than a concept or belief system. She spent her life learning about him and getting to know his steady character, and how he interacted with people. She talked to him and sang to him, laughed and cried with him. It was an easy matter to take her requests to God, and a gift from him would certainly be recognized—and trusted in his care.

A worthy goal it would be for a woman to have a Hannah-like relationship with God. Imagine how that kind of communion with the God of universe— to recognize him, to see his gifts—would change your days. What peace would be poured into Your Life as you trusted yourself, and all he gives, into his hands for his beautiful and sacred purposes.

You, Lord, give true peace to those who depend on you, because they trust you.

Isaiah 26:3 NCV

Samuel, which means "name of God," was Hannah's answer to prayer. David Guzik, in his *Enduring Word Commentary* series, uses this idea to translate "lending":

"Literally, 'I also have lent him to the LORD' could be translated, 'And I also made myself to ask him for the LORD.' The idea is not that Hannah 'owns' the child and is 'lending' him to the LORD. Instead, the idea is that the child is her 'prayer,' or the fulfillment of her prayer to the LORD."

Hannah found it easy to dedicate her son into service for God. Charles Spurgeon, in one of his *Morning and Evening* devotions, said:

"Hannah's one heaven-given child was dearer far, because he was the fruit of earnest pleadings. . . . That which we win by prayer we should dedicate to God, as Hannah dedicated Samuel. The gift came from heaven, let it go to heaven. Prayer brought it; gratitude sang over it; let devotion consecrate it."

Zooming **In**

Shiloh, the secluded city where Eli and Hannah worshipped, was Israel's first capital and remained so for 369 years. About the time the nation turned to the rule of kings, the Philistines attacked Shiloh. It was later burned to the ground. The area today is called Khirbet Seilun. Within the last twenty-five years, a layer of ash was discovered by academic archaeologists. They've confirmed that it was from an ancient fire consistent with how the Bible describes the destruction of Shiloh. The name Shiloh is difficult to translate, but is often taken to mean "tranquillity," or "resting place." Some Jews have returned to live there.

To Hannah, God was so near, so trustworthy, that giving Samuel into his care was barely giving him up at all. Imagine that kind of closeness to God.

What is something you've received from God through your earnest pleadings? How might you keep your heart grateful, and your hands open, to God's use of it?

_____

_____

_____

_____

Consider the talents and gifts you've been given—singing, cooking, gardening, teaching. How do you imagine these being used for God's beautiful and sacred purposes?

_____

_____

_____

Hannah cherished Samuel, and she wanted the best for him. What is something you cherish? What "best" do you see for it as you freely give it into God's trustworthy hands?

_____

_____

_____

Looking in All the Wrong Places

God remembered Rachel. He listened to her and opened her womb. She conceived and bore a son, and said, "God has taken away my shame." She named him Joseph: "May the Lord add another son to me."

Genesis 30:22–24 HCSB

The Big Picture

Two wives do not make a happy home, as you can imagine, but having two or more was common in Rachel's day. Her husband, Jacob, had married her sister, Leah, first. Not by his choice, but that's another story. Needless to say, two sisters living under the same roof and vying for the same husband's attention spelled trouble from the start. Also, bearing children was highly valued at that time, and it seemed to create a contest. The wife with the most, or any at all, considered herself more honored. In this family, Leah had children, and Rachel had none. But Rachel had her husband's love, and Leah did not. What a mess.

Leah had four sons in succession. Their given names reflected her hope that God would hear her, and Jacob would love her. She named the first Reuben, meaning "look, I have a son." The second she named "Simeon," meaning "hearing," because God had *heard* that she was unloved. Levi was third. His name meant "attached," for Leah hoped now that she had given

take a CLOSER look for women

Jacob three sons, he would finally become attached to her. Judah meant "celebrated," for Leah now had four sons to win her husband's love.

For Rachel, the shame of not having any children was too much. She went to Jacob and said, "If you don't give me children, I will die." Maybe a bit melodramatic. Jacob thought so. He became angry and told her that he could do nothing about it; it was up to God.

Rachel pleaded, "Then go sleep with my maid, and her children can be mine." He did, and her maid, Bilhah, had two sons, Dan and Naphtali, meaning "judge" and "wrestling." Leah decided to send Jacob to her maid, Zilpah. She had two sons whom Leah named Gad and Asher—"good fortune" and "happy."

One day, Reuben, Leah's first child, brought in mandrakes from the field. These were a potato-like fruit that Rachel superstitiously believed would give her a child. She bargained with Leah for some of them, and Leah agreed— only if Jacob would sleep with her. He did, and she bore two more sons, Issachar and Zebulun, meaning "reward" and "dwelling."

Of course the mandrakes were powerless, but God listened to Rachel and gave her a child. She no longer felt ashamed. She gave birth to Joseph and hoped God would grant her another son.

Be still, and in the quiet moments, listen to the voice of your heavenly Father. His words can renew your spirit . . . no one knows you and your needs like He does.

Janet L. Weaver

In this story, Rachel and Leah's rivalry stands out. Many feel that Rachel only continued to demand her way. If you look closer, however, there are signs of change in Rachel's heart toward God. Somewhere along the way, a surrender took place.

Rachel envied, begged, whined, and bargained, but she must have begun to pray. God *listened* to Rachel. In response she was given Joseph. His name is made up of two Hebrew words, *Asaph* and *Yasaph*. The first means "to take away," and the second "to add to." Rachel believed God took away her shame and would add the blessing of another child.

Rachel also expressed this belief in the names she used for God. First is *Elohim*—mighty God, Creator of the universe who exists as the Father, the Son, and the Holy Spirit. It is he who created the child within Rachel and removed her shame of childlessness. Then Rachel said that Jehovah would bring to her another son. Jehovah, meaning "self-existent one," was the most sacred name used for God. In spite of all Rachel's previous actions, you see here a glimmer of full belief and trust taking root in her heart.

> *Unanswered yet? Nay, do not say ungranted; perhaps your part is not yet wholly done; the work began when first your prayer was uttered, and God will finish what He has begun.*
>
> Ophelia Adams

The longings of a woman's heart reach deep. Whether it is a yearning for a child, a special relationship, a sense of purpose, or even approval, unfulfilled desires can become all-consuming. "If I don't get this, I will die," Rachel said. In desperation, she devised her own solutions, but none yielded what she sought. Somewhere along the way she began to consider God's love for her, and to trust her desires into his hands.

You have natural longings unique to you as a woman. You also have beliefs about God's participation in bringing about their fulfillment. God is involved. He cares deeply about you and what you long for. He also knows what you need. Your growing assurance of his goodwill for you can help you rest, and wait, for his timing and his plans.

No, you won't need mandrakes or any other special ingredients—just a willing heart that is growing in trust of the one who wants what is good and lovely for you. Ask him. Trust him. Involve him. Rest in him.

This is the confidence we have in approaching God: that if we ask anything according to his will, he hears us.

1 John 5:14 NIV

Rachel's trust in God grew, and at the right time, she had a child. Albert Barnes discussed this in his *Notes on the Bible*:

"'God remembered Rachel,' in the best time for her, after he had taught her the lessons of dependence and patience. 'Joseph.' There is a remote allusion to her gratitude for the reproach of barrenness taken away. But there is also hope in the name. The selfish feeling also has died away, and the thankful Rachel rises from Elohim, the invisible Eternal, to Yahweh, the manifest Self-existent."

Rachel expressed thanks for God's mercy and hope for another son in her naming of Joseph. Matthew Henry, in *Matthew Henry's Commentary of the Whole Bible,* explained it this way:

"She takes this mercy as an earnest of further mercy. 'Has God given me his grace? I may call it Joseph, and say, He shall add more grace! Has he given me his joy? I may call it Joseph, and say, He will give me more joy. Has he begun, and shall he not make an end?'"

Zooming **In**

In the winter, mandrakes bear blue flowers, which turn into a small, light-orange fruit in the summertime. Women in Rachel's time believed the pleasantly fragrant fruit helped barren women to conceive. It has sometimes been called the "love apple." It grows in different parts of Palestine, including Jerusalem.

Traditionally Jehovah, the proper name of the God of Israel, has been considered sacred to the Jewish people, and so it was not pronounced. Until the time of the Renaissance, the divine name was written without vowels: YHWH. Later the vowels of another name for God, Adonai, were added to help in the pronunciation.

As long as Rachel focused on Leah, she was unable to yield her heart's desire to God. Once she turned her eyes toward him, he opened the floodgates of blessing toward her.

Through the
Eyes of
Your Heart

Competition and jealousy have a way of getting under a woman's skin. Do you see any signs of them in your life? How might you let go of these feelings and trust God with your goals?

_____

_____

_____

Rachel tried all kinds of ways to get what she wanted. Nothing worked—except trusting God. What are your deepest longings? Yield those into God's loving hands.

_____

_____

_____

God knows your needs and desires better than anyone. Can you believe that? How will that change how you interact with your friends, family, and coworkers?

_____

_____

_____

_____

Never Give Up

> *When they couldn't find a way in because of the crowd, they went up on the roof, removed some tiles, and let him down in the middle of everyone, right in front of Jesus. Impressed by their bold belief, he said, "Friend, I forgive your sins."*
>
> Luke 5:19–20 MSG

The Big Picture

Word spread quickly. Jesus was in Peter's house teaching. Many who wanted to see him were already crowding into the house. Jewish religious leaders had traveled from all over Galilee and as far away as Judea. Jesus had recently preached in the synagogues of Galilee and healed a leper. What would he do next?

In a nearby neighborhood a few men lifted their paralyzed friend onto a cot. Perhaps Jesus would heal him, too. "You two pick up that side, and the two of us will get this side," one might have said. "One, two, three . . . lift," and off they went toward Peter's house.

As they approached, they found a wall of people surrounding the doorway and packing into the courtyard of the house where Jesus was speaking. They considered the roof route. This is how they might have done it:

Two of the men took some rope and climbed up outer steps to the roof. With the help of the other two, they used their ropes like a pulley to draw the

take a CLOSER look for women

cot up to the roof. In the middle of the terrace was a square covered with tiles. This square covered an opening during the rainy season, and at other times, was set aside to let light and air into the courtyard below.

The men carefully laid aside the tiles, and then lowered their friend right in front of Jesus. You can picture the amazement and smile on the teacher's face. He realized the faith, not only of the man who was laid before him, but also of the four men whose heads were peeking through the opening above.

"Son," he told the paralyzed man, "your offenses are forgiven."

The religious leaders were outraged. *Only God forgives sins,* they thought to themselves.

Jesus knew what they were thinking. He asked them, "Would it be easier to tell him his sins are forgiven, or to tell him to get up and walk?" Then, to show that he had both the power to forgive and to heal, he told the man to get up and return to his house. The paralytic man did just that. He took his bed and left the house.

At Peter's house Jesus declared, through his actions and his words, he was God in the flesh come to heal not only infirmities of the flesh, but also those of the soul.

The tragedies that now blacken and darken the very air of heaven for us, will sink into their places in a scheme so august, so magnificent, so joyful, that we shall laugh for wonder and delight.

Arthur Christopher Bacon

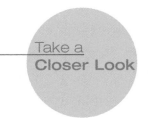

It's exciting to get together with other women and find innovative solutions for problems. The paralyzed man certainly had creative friends. Many had crowded into the house in Capernaum to see Jesus, but notice, none were quite as persistent as the little band of men who brought their paralyzed friend. They were determined to do whatever it took to get near Jesus.

You can almost picture these four sitting around their disabled friend's home with him, talking about Jesus' visit to their town. The planning and determination began long before they arrived at the courthouse of Peter's home. So did the faith it took to believe that every effort they made would bring them closer to the results they sought—the healing of their friend.

Notice also that Jesus was impressed with their persistence. Based on the faith of *all* of them, he healed the paralyzed man. The Greek word for *faith* used here is *pistis*, which means "firm persuasion, conviction, belief in the truth." That faith was the force behind the determination and boldness of these friends. It was their inspiration to refuse to be deterred. They were wonderfully rewarded by their creativity—their friend was healed physically and spiritually.

> *Firmness of purpose is one of the most necessary sinews of character, and one of the best instruments of success.*
>
> Philip Dormer Chesterfield

The enthusiasm, persistence, and creativity of those four friends is inspiring. They loved their friend and would do whatever it took to help him. Wouldn't it have been fun to grab an edge of the paralytic's pallet and go along for the adventure? In some ways you can.

Every time you talk on the phone with a friend who needs advice, get together for tea with a coworker who is struggling, or invite someone out for a getaway shopping trip, you can be grabbing an edge of the pallet. You're connecting with others to encourage them—maybe even bringing them nearer to Jesus.

Get creative. But also realize you may come up against a few obstacles. Refuse to be deterred. When one way to encourage or help your friend doesn't work, try another. And remember, it takes more than one person to carry a pallet. Ask your hurting friend who else she'd like to have come alongside.

Have fun with this adventure. And don't be too surprised if you all end up face-to-face—or heart-to-heart—with Jesus.

By helping each other with your troubles, you truly obey the law of Christ.

Galatians 6:2 NCV

How Others
See It

The paralytic's friends were certainly determined. J. C. Ryle, in *Expository Thoughts on Luke,* offered this thought on seeking to draw nearer to God:

"In all our endeavors to draw near to God, in all our approaches to Christ, there ought to be the same determined earnestness which was shown by this sick man's friends. We must allow no difficulties to check us, and no obstacle to keep us back from anything which is really for our spiritual good."

The creativity and attitude of the crippled man and his friends were amazing. This is noted by authors William Hendricksen and Simon J. Kistemaker in *New Testament Commentary–Luke*:

"The courage and resourcefulness of all five—the paralytic plus his four helpers—particularly also their faith in the success of their venture, hence ultimately their trust in Jesus, must be admired. . . . The confidence of the five touched the very heart of Jesus, who now, in accents tender yet firm, said to the paralytic, 'Man, your sins are forgiven you.'"

Zooming **In**

Just like porches and decks today, rooftops of ancient Jewish homes could be extensions of the family's living quarters. A stair outside the home, or from the court, led up to a flat roof. The roof, made of brick or stone, was often sloped to allow for drainage of rain. Jewish law required that the roof had a strong balustrade, or rail, at least three feet high. The roof space was used as a cool and airy place for the family to gather, or as a place to escape for quiet or prayer. A guest room might be built on the roof to offer privacy to the guest and the family.

Tenacity and creativity, like that seen in the friends of the paralytic, are some of the most delightful ingredients of a good friendship; and, oh, the glorious outcome when they're put into action.

Tenacity keeps you hopeful and undeterred. Where, in your life right now, do you need a measure of this quality?

_____

_____

_____

Creative determination encourages everyone around you. Is there a way you can use this to come alongside a friend and help her carry her pallet?

_____

_____

_____

_____

Do you enjoy using your creativity to decorate, experiment with meals, or add personal touches to your workspace? What are ways you can use this to cheer a friend?

_____

_____

_____

Delightful Generosity

Sitting across from the temple treasury, He watched how the crowd dropped money into the treasury. Many rich people were putting in large sums. And a poor widow came and dropped in two tiny coins worth very little.

Mark 12:41–42 HCSB

The Big Picture

It was Tuesday of the week that has come to be known as the Passion Week—the last days of Jesus' life on earth. This particular day was full for Jesus. Every action he took, every word he said, had intense meaning; but perhaps, in that one way, it wasn't that different from any other day of his powerful life.

The morning began with a walk toward the temple of Jerusalem. As Jesus and his disciples came near the temple, the Jewish religious leaders and teachers saw him. They had witnessed Jesus send away the people who were selling their wares in the temple area the day before. They had also seen him heal the sick, and had heard his teachings about God. Here was their chance to challenge him, perhaps trick him, and get him in trouble or arrested.

Over the next few moments, Jesus calmly listened to their questions. Some he did not answer, or, in return, he asked them questions. Other times he told them stories. He did this so they would consider, from their own knowledge of Scriptures, who he was—God's Son, even the Messiah that their ancestor

David had talked about. And they could also think more deeply about who they were—teachers who burdened the people with their ideas, unable to live up to their own high standards themselves. He warned them, taught them, and challenged them.

Then he pulled aside by himself near the temple treasury. For a while he watched as the people came and gave money for the temple, the priests, or the poor. Each giver cast their coins into one or several of thirteen chests. The offering was to be given voluntarily. Jesus watched many of the rich give large sums. Then a poor widow approached and dropped in two *prutahs*, the smallest sum allowed.

He turned to his disciples who were standing near by. "Come over here," he said. When they came, he told them, "I want to show you an important truth. This poor widow gave more than all the others who are throwing their coins into the treasury. They gave from their extra money, but she gave all she had, even what could keep her alive."

No other words were recorded from this conversation—no response from the disciples, no explanation from Jesus. Perhaps none were needed. It was clear the poor woman gave all she had. Her tiny gift became the greatest given that day.

A generous person will be enriched, and the one who gives a drink of water will receive water.

Proverbs 11:25 HCSB

Gifts from the heart, no matter how small, bring joy. At the temple, Jesus noticed one who gave such a gift. Look closely at the situation through his eyes. He watched, not to judge, but to find delight in the one who gave all she had.

"Come here, I want to show you something," Jesus might have said to his disciples. You can almost imagine the excitement in his voice over the joy he wanted to share. He had watched for a long time. Many had come and gone. Those who were rich likely dropped coins in several of the thirteen boxes to designate where the money was to be spent. They gave out of their plenty, their *perisseuso*. This word is Hebrew for "excess," their "leftover" money.

He draws attention to these givers, not with condemnation, but as a point of contrast—for there came the widow who had no excess, no leftover anything. Somehow Jesus knows that she gave every bit of what she had. Most of all, he knows her heart. She gave those two frail coins with the deepest sense of gratitude and worship toward God. She gave them fully trusting that he would take care of her needs. She gave them with love.

> *Let us seek the spirit of the poor widow, who knew that God could do without her gift, but felt that her love could not be satisfied without her sacrifice.*
>
> A. Rowland

What beautiful devotion this poor widow showed toward God. What utter trust. Perhaps you're not a poor woman at all, but you can be like her.

Apply It
to Your Life

Of course you might look for ways you have plenty and then give more generously, but for a moment consider something else. In what ways do you feel a lack, as if you're just barely surviving? Where in your life do you feel *poor*?

Maybe it is an inability to talk freely to others, to offer a minute or two of the right words of comfort. Maybe it's a lack of energy, or time, or skill. Maybe you'd like to invite people over, but feel your home lacks what others have. Maybe you've wanted to help in the community, or the church, but feel others might laugh at you.

Like the poor woman, take what you have, no matter how tiny or seemingly worthless. Make it a gift of your heart, a way to show God you love him. Give it all. Give with abandoned joy. In God's eyes, your gift is a treasure and a delight.

The Lord sees not as man sees: man looks on the outward appearance, but the Lord looks on the heart.

1 Samuel 16:7 ESV

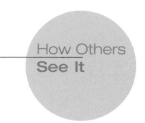

The heart of the giver is what delighted Jesus. David Guzik, in *David Guzik's Commentaries on the Bible,* points out part of the reason why:

"Jesus' principle here shows us that God does not need our money. If God needed our money, then *how much* we give would be more important than our *heart* in giving. Instead, it is *our* privilege to give to Him, and we need to give because it is good for us, not because it is good for God."

In "Homilies by A. Rowland" in the section on Mark in *The Pulpit Commentary,* A. Rowland talked about Jesus' view of the offerings at the temple:

"We may put into the treasury wealth, talents, prayers, tears, etc. None are unnoticed by him. And he looks in order to approve, not to condemn. . . . He saw the pious intention, the pure purpose, and out of all the chaff on that threshing floor, he found one grain of purity and reality, and rejoiced over it as one finding great spoil."

Zooming **In**

Prutahs, the Hebrew name for the coins the widow gave, is often translated "mite" because it had the smallest value among coins. They were thin and made of inferior bronze or copper. Because they deteriorated easily, few coins from this time have been found. Jews used pictures of religion and culture on coins to avoid breaking the commandment that forbade graven images of men or idols. One coin, found from the time of 69–40 BC, has a sun with eight rays representing the "sun of righteousness," or the Messiah of Malachi 4:2, on one side, while on the other side, a ship's anchor symbolized God's steadfast promises.

What a joy it is to have what you see as a lack, but like the poor woman, to give it all away in delightful generosity and gratefulness to God.

Through the
Eyes of
Your Heart

The poor widow didn't worry about what she would have left. Where do you feel poor and lacking? Think of some creative ways you can turn your "lack" into a generous gift.

_____

_____

_____

Gratitude was beautifully expressed in the widow's offering. Look around your home, even with all it seems to lack. How can you use it as a thank offering to God?

_____

_____

_____

A small gift of time, a simply decorated note, a smile, these are little ways to begin giving generously to others. What might you try to do this week?

_____

_____

_____

_____

A Peculiar Joy

God will bless you when people insult you, mistreat you, and tell all kinds of evil lies about you because of me. Be happy and excited! You will have a great reward in heaven. People did these same things to the prophets who lived long ago.

Matthew 5:11–12 CEV

The Big Picture

During the summertime, in the mountains near Galilee, Jesus gave a message that has become known as the Sermon on the Mount. A large number had gathered from all over the region. Some came out of curiosity, but most were his followers. In their eyes, he was the Messiah come to establish his earthly kingdom. In this sermon, Jesus began to turn their ideas about the kingdom upside down.

Jesus sat down, looked into the eyes of those who loved him, and taught them principles, not of the earthly kingdom, but of God's kingdom as it should be lived out on earth. "Blessed are you," he began as he taught them about humility, passion, integrity, and love.

Then he said, "Blessed are all those who are persecuted for saying and doing what is right in God's eyes. These possess all the joy and peace of God's eternal kingdom." Perhaps Jesus paused before his next statement, for he meant it to be extremely personal to his listeners: "Blessed are *you* when

take a CLOSER look for women

you are insulted and mistreated because of what you do for me. Be glad and leap for joy when this happens, for you will be rewarded in heaven. Think of all the prophets before your time who went through the very same thing. You aren't alone."

Not alone. As Jesus spoke, images of the ancient prophets likely came to mind. Isaiah, Jeremiah, and others who declared God's truths and who were ridiculed, slandered, or ignored; Elijah, who ran for his life from the evil Queen Jezebel; many prophets who were put to death, often by their own people, for their bold willingness to say what God told them to say. Would Jesus' listeners face such extreme rejection and persecution as this? At that moment, it might have seemed unlikely.

In those beginning thoughts of his sermon, Jesus laid a foundation for a new way of living with one another and in one's relationship with God. It clearly wouldn't be easy, but he taught that those who followed this way would be greatly blessed. Soon enough, those who listened and chose to follow him as his disciples would understand what Jesus meant and how difficult it would be to live it out—*and* stay alive.

Joy in affliction is rooted in the hope of resurrection, but our experience of suffering also deepens the root of that hope.

John Piper

Jesus' "blessed are you" teachings were also known as the *Beatitudes,* from the Latin *beatus*—"supreme blessedness." Each addressed a specific virtue and, as a whole, were Jesus' declarations of blessedness. But look closely. His last one presented a difficult paradox: be exceedingly glad in the face of horrible treatment.

The meaning of *blessed* as Jesus used it goes much deeper than "happiness." It is *markarios* in Greek and refers to "a state marked by fullness in God," or "blessed one—possessing the favor of God." It is a lifestyle perspective: a person's spiritual connection to God would be their source of fullness and satisfaction, not their circumstances.

That went for any insults or persecution his listeners would experience *because* of their belief in him. In these they were to "rejoice" and be "exceedingly glad"—be ecstatic. Why? Theirs *is* the kingdom of heaven—that blessed fullness in God, the position as a favored child— right now and forever. Jesus focused their attention on the eternal—heaven's rewards—for when they faced difficulties on his behalf, it mattered eternally. Knowing all this, they could leap for joy, even when mistreated and persecuted.

> *Let us not be surprised when we have to face difficulties. When the wind blows hard on a tree, the roots stretch and grow the stronger. Let it be so with us. Let us not be weaklings, yielding to every wind that blows, but strong in spirit to resist.*
>
> Amy Carmichael

In many places in the world, women of the Christian faith receive harsh treatment. Some are even killed. The persecution you face as woman is likely not dangerous like this, but it is present. It is subtle.

The freedom to openly share or live your faith as a Christian is narrowing all the time. As a woman, however, you might have noticed other difficulties. In some situations, biblical values for women—like femininity, purity, and gentleness—are becoming less and less valued. The more you are willing to be crass and tolerant, the more likely you will be accepted. On the other hand, when you take a stance, you're labeled "straitlaced," "naive," or "boring."

Jesus knew that he was asking for a commitment to an unusual way of life, and he knew those who followed it would be opposed—possibly hated, insulted, or persecuted. In living the life he teaches, you might experience insults and suffering, but you'll also know deep joy.

Focus on Jesus, who endured the same. How did he respond? He remained firm in his convictions. He kept a steady eye on his Father God and the eternal purpose for his life. Remember, you are his daughter, and you are blessed.

Our momentary light affliction is producing for us an absolutely incomparable eternal weight of glory.

2 Corinthians 4:17 HCSB

It is devotion to Jesus that brings the possibility of persecution and also the promise of blessing. Martin Luther, in *Luther's Commentary on Galatians,* made this clear when he said:

"We know that we suffer these things not because we are thieves and murderers, but for Christ's sake whose Gospel we proclaim. We have no reason to complain. The world, of course, looks upon us as unhappy and accursed creatures, but Christ for whose sake we suffer pronounces us blessed and bids us to rejoice. 'Blessed are ye,' says He."

David Guzik, in his Enduring Word Commentary series, encouraged his readers to consider the values expressed in the Beatitudes:

"Why will the world persecute them? Because the values and character expressed in these Beatitudes are so opposite to the world's manner of thinking. Our persecution may not be much compared to others, but if *no one* speaks evil of you, are these Beatitudes traits of your life?"

Zooming **In**

Jesus' sermon took place on a hill near Capernaum, most likely on the road between Nazareth and Tiberias. The hill most often claimed as the correct site is called Kuran Huttin or "the Horns of Huttin." It is rocky and steep, has two hills, or horns, with a flatter area between them.

Persecution of Christians began shortly after Jesus' sermon and included women. Before Paul became one of Jesus' apostles, he hated Christians. He had many bound, imprisoned, and stoned to death—including women. Today, in some countries where persecution for one's beliefs is common, Christian women can be arrested, abandoned, beaten, or worse.

> *Blessedness is a lifestyle perspective of being in relationship with God as one of his own. It's living the way Jesus taught regardless of what it costs.*

God meant for you to enjoy and protect who you are as a woman—the beauty of who you are inside, your purity, your femininity. Describe yourself as God's beloved daughter.

_____

_____

_____

Women, masquerading as objects, demolish the image God meant for them to enjoy. What pressures do you face to conform to your culture and your peers? How might you stand against them?

_____

_____

_____

Your growing relationship with God softens the insults that life hurls at you. It focuses on what you have with him for eternity. Write out what you're learning, so it will help you through the difficult moments.

_____

_____

_____

A Gift of Friendship

When David finished talking with Saul, Jonathan felt very close to David. He loved David as much as he loved himself. Saul kept David with him from that day on and did not let him go home to his father's house. Jonathan made an agreement with David, because he loved David as much as himself. He took off his coat and gave it to David, along with his armor, including his sword, bow, and belt.

1 Samuel 18:1–4 NCV

The
Big Picture

Young David lived in Israel under the rule of a king named Saul. He was a shepherd and a gifted musician. Sometimes, when the king was depressed, David was summoned to play the lyre for him. He likely never imagined he would someday become king.

One day the Philistines had gathered to attack Israel. David's three oldest brothers were sent to battle. David's father asked him to take food to them. "Go to your brothers. Bring back something to show they are safe." The next morning David rose early to go to his brothers.

When he arrived, the battle was beginning. A Philistine giant named Goliath was shouting at the Israelites, "Give me a man to fight against." All of Saul's men were frightened.

Thinking, *This Philistine can't disregard the armies of the living God*, David wanted to challenge this giant.

Saul heard about David's bravery, and he called for him. "You are young. What can you do against this man who has battled all his life?"

take a CLOSER look for women

"As a shepherd, I've rescued my father's sheep from lions and bears. God, who delivered me then, will keep me safe from this Philistine."

Saul offered his armor, but David went forward with only his staff, a sling, and five smooth stones. The giant mocked and cursed the young shepherd. David wasn't afraid. "I come to you in the name of the God of Israel whom you've insulted. He will deliver you into my hands and all will know that God saves, not by sword or spear."

The two ran toward each other. David reached into his pouch for a stone and, using his sling, shot the giant, hitting him in the forehead and killing him. The Israelites finished the battle and defeated the Philistines.

Though David had played the lyre for him, King Saul had not recognized the shepherd. His commander brought David to Saul, and for some time they talked. Saul put David into full service in his courts, and in charge of one of his troops.

Jonathan, Saul's son, was there too. As he listened to the conversation, he greatly admired David, even loved him as his own soul. He made a covenant of friendship with David by taking off his royal attire and armor, and giving it to his new friend.

David trusted God for his protection and the victory over the Philistines. He was honored for his courage, and became successful wherever Saul sent him.

Friendship is a comforting smile, a familiar voice that warms the heart, and the freedom to be the person God intended.

Author Unknown

A healthy friendship is like a skillfully woven, knitted garment—warm and strong.

Through a victory, God positioned David to someday be king, but he also gave him a strong friend. Look at Jonathan's actions. He showed balanced self-acceptance and humility in that he loved David "as himself."

The details of the conversation between Saul and David aren't recorded, only Jonathan's response. His actions show more than admiration for a courageous act. His loving David as himself shows he immediately felt a connection and commonality with the shepherd. Together they made a mutual pact of friendship.

Removing his royal robe, armor, and sword, Jonathan honored his new friend with these symbols of nobility he stripped from himself. He symbolically marked the beginning of a lifetime commitment to his friend. Whether aware or not, the prince gave the future king royal attire. His willingness to have David wear it shows how deeply he trusted his own future to God, and how highly he valued his friendship with David.

It was a beautiful act done to secure what was more important to Jonathan than the trappings of notoriety or lofty aspirations—friendship.

> *We need not set out in search for a friend . . . rather, we must simply set out to be the friend Christ modeled—anticipating the needs of others, wearing ourselves out at giving.*
>
> Joy MacKenzie

When you look closely at a knitted garment, you see steady, interlocking stitches made from a continuous thin string of yarn. When completed, the piece is sturdy and strong. It can be pulled and stretched, and it won't unravel. Such was the nature of Jonathan and David's friendship.

Apply It
to Your Life

A friend like Jonathan is a rare and beautiful find—something to long for, something to be. In Jonathan you see no signs of an ulterior motive—just sincerity and a willingness to set aside any pretenses. Without losing site of who God created him to be, he committed himself to David. No matter what happened in the future, he would remain a steadfast friend. You could trust someone like Jonathan. That's a healthy friendship, gracefully knit in genuineness and integrity.

Maybe you long for that kind of friend—someone you can share the depths of your soul with; someone you can trust not just today or tomorrow, but for years to come. Ask God to bring a Jonathan into your life. Ask him to help you be that kind of friend for others.

Now that you have purified your souls by your obedience to the truth so that you have genuine mutual love, love one another deeply from the heart.

1 Peter 1:22 NRSV

Pride had no place in Jonathan and David's friendship. Matthew Henry, in *Matthew Henry's Concise Commentary of the Bible,* focused on David's humility:

"The friendship of David and Jonathan was the effect of Divine grace, which produces in true believers one heart and one soul, and causes them to love each other. . . . Where God unites hearts, carnal matters are too weak to separate them. . . . It was certainly a great proof of the power of God's grace in David, that he was able to bear all this respect and honour, without being lifted up above measure."

Jonathan's gesture of giving his robe and armor carried great significance. David Roper, in his sermon "Jonathan and David," said:

"My friend is the person who has a need, and whose need I can meet by pouring out my soul to him. . . . It is symbolized here in verse 4, in Jonathan's stripping himself of his robe and giving it to David, even including his sword and his bow and his belt. . . . Jonathan provided whatever his need was. The result was that David became successful."

Zooming **In**

Goliath's size was six cubits and a span. A cubit was about twenty-one inches, and a span was half a cubit. This giant David slew was at least eleven feet, four inches tall. There were other giants this size and larger. Pliny, the historian, wrote of Ethiopians, called Syrobotae, who were eight cubits high.

In the time of Jonathan and David, friend's exchanged armor to express that they were giving of themselves. An ancient Akkadian document records a thirteenth-century king who divorced his wife. When the son chose to go with his mother, he gave up his right to the throne. The boy demonstrated his choice, symbolically, by leaving his clothing on the throne.

Jonathan loved David and gave of himself—even when it meant David's advancement over his own. Trust God with your friendships and your future.

Through the
Eyes of
Your Heart

Sometimes all that is required to set aside for your friend is a few moments to hear her struggles. How might you tenderly nurture one of your friendships simply through listening?

_____

_____

_____

Do you enjoy how God made you? Growing in accepting yourself will help you knit stronger friendships. What are some things you accept about yourself? What are some things you need to grow to accept?

_____

_____

_____

What are ways in which you have sacrificed for a friend? Ways you might in the future? How will you do these and still allow *both* you and your friend to be all God meant for you to be?

_____

_____

_____

Recognizing Jesus

"They have taken my Lord away," she said, "and I don't know where they have put him." At this, she turned around and saw Jesus standing there, but she did not realize that it was Jesus. "Woman," he said, "why are you crying? Who is it you are looking for?"

John 20:13–15 NIV

The Big Picture

The tears were those of Mary of Magdala, a woman consumed by grief over the death of a loved one. You have felt that grief, or known others who have. Closure helps ease the pain. Things must be finished. Mary desperately felt the need for closure as she sought to complete the burial preparations for Jesus' body. She loved him deeply.

Her return to Jesus' tomb after his death on the cross is a passion-filled glimpse into the heart of one of his devoted followers. All four Gospels give an account of the women who visited Jesus' grave. Only John's Gospel gives a personal view of Mary's distress when she discovered the empty tomb.

Earlier in his travels, Jesus had cured Mary of demonic possession. She then chose to go with Jesus and, along with several other women, support his and his disciples' ministry. When the Roman soldiers later snatched Jesus from them, and the people killed him on the cross, imagine how their world turned upside down.

Jesus died on a Friday with sunset fast approaching. The Sabbath would soon be upon them, and until sunset the next evening, no work could be done. Sabbath was a time of rest, an important Jewish observance of a cherished covenant with God. It couldn't be broken, even for the burial of a loved one. A proper burial for Jesus seemed impossible.

But then a man named Joseph offered his own tomb where he and others laid Jesus' body. Keeping with the custom of burying a body with honor, the women went home to prepare spices and perfumes. They would go back Sunday morning to finish the burial. Before light broke that Sunday morning, Mary returned to the tomb, her heart as heavy as the darkness that shrouded the pathways. But she had to finish.

She arrived to find the stone pushed away from the entrance. Jesus was gone. Did they take him away? Alarmed, Mary rushed to find the disciples. They returned with her, but they had no answers, and left her weeping at the tomb. She wasn't comforted by the disciples or by the angels sitting inside. When the resurrected Jesus stood by her, she mistook him for a gardener. He said her name, "Mary," and she finally realized who he was. Mary was one of the first to witness Jesus alive, and she was filled with joy.

The beautiful thing about this adventure called faith is that we can count on Him never to lead us astray.

Charles R. Swindoll

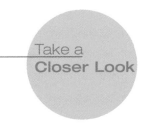

It's interesting that Mary didn't recognize Jesus when he was standing right in front of her. Why didn't she, when even in her travels with him, he had revealed so much? Had she missed his assurances that even with the coming events she would see him again?

"My hour is come." "I'm going away to him who sent me." "I will not leave you as orphans." "You have sorrow now, but I will see you again." "No one can rob you of your joy."

But the Cross happened, the unexpected horror of torture and death. This couldn't have been his plan. It seemed Mary believed he was gone forever. She went to the tomb to finish burial preparations.

Jesus could have revealed himself when she first arrived. Instead, he allowed Mary's journey of discovery. She moved from thinking Jesus' body had been taken away, to seeing him right in front of her; from not recognizing him, to finally seeing that he was there, and that he is Lord. It wasn't a game. Jesus lovingly led Mary toward the truth, and she moved from sorrow into joy.

> *Faith never knows where it is being led, but it loves and knows the One who is leading.*
>
> Oswald Chambers

When traumatic events crash into your life, the emotions can feel consuming. The hope and happiness of previous days are seemingly gone. It all happens so fast. It's hard to know what to do. Mary must have been the kind of person who responded to such events by getting busy, by doing something to set things at least a little right. But Mary lost sight of Jesus, even to the point of not recognizing him when he stood right in front of her.

Apply It
to Your Life

It can happen to you, too, for sorrow has a way of veiling sound perspective. And what gets left on the side you can see seems so convincing. "Jesus is gone," Mary said.

In those moments, know that what Jesus did with Mary, he does with you, too. He gradually takes you through your questions and misconceptions to a place of greater understanding. He does not leave you alone or in the dark. At the right time, he shows himself to you. He does all this within a loving relationship—one in which he calls you by name, and invites you to look into his face. What will you see? He is there.

May the God of hope fill you with all joy and peace in believing, so that you may overflow with hope by the power of the Holy Spirit.

Romans 15:13 HCSB

In her anxiety, Mary lost track of what she knew was true about God. Perhaps she reminds you of someone you know. In the sermon "The Incredible Hope" from his book *God's Loving Word,* Ray Stedman said:

"Mary was just like us! Have you ever found yourself in a distressing circumstance, when the sky seemed to come crashing down on you, and Christian that you are, you immediately forgot all the promises of God? You felt sorry for yourself; you became anxious and upset. I have. We so quickly forget the promises of God.

"Martin Luther once spent three days in a black depression over something that had gone wrong. On the third day his wife came downstairs dressed in mourning clothes. 'Who's dead?' he asked her. 'God,' she replied. Luther rebuked her, saying, 'What do you mean, God is dead? God cannot die.' 'Well,' she replied, 'the way you've been acting I was sure He had!'

"Many of us have been caught in that trap. This is also what happened to Mary."

Zooming **In**

When Jesus said *woman,* he meant it as a term of courtesy and warmth. Culturally, it was a man's world in Jesus' time, but his treatment and views of women were different from those of other men of his day. Many godly women were influential in his life. Mary of Magdala was one of them.

The Jews didn't embalm their dead or use caskets; instead, they washed and anointed the bodies with spices, such as aloe and myrrh, and then wrapped them in strips of cloth. Tombs in Jesus' time were natural caves or chambers, cut from the stone cliffs. A ledge along the opening held a large stone door that weighed from one to three tons.

> *Jesus wasn't gone forever as Mary thought. He was still there. He is with you now in your present circumstances. Do you recognize him?*

In a deep loss or difficult situation, have you found yourself doubting God's presence? What were some of your questions?

_____

_____

_____

_____

Consider any misconceptions you might have about God that would keep you from recognizing that he is with you. What has he shown you about himself that will help you see him clearly and truthfully?

_____

_____

_____

Remember those moments when God showed you how much he loves you? How can they help you the next time you struggle with believing he is with you?

_____

_____

_____

_____

Come Yet Closer

Job arose, tore his robe, and shaved his head; and he fell to the ground and worshiped. And he said: "Naked I came from my mother's womb, and naked shall I return there. The LORD gave, and the LORD has taken away; blessed be the name of the LORD."

Job 1:20–21 NKJV

The Big Picture

The curtain rose on the first act of the story of Job—set partly in heaven, partly on earth. By the time this drama had played out, Job discovered depths of God he never imagined. Look at the opening scenes.

Off to one side of the giant stage of the universe, Job busily interacted with his wife and their ten children. They, along with his many workers, helped him manage his immense land and herds of thousands of animals. He was known as a man of integrity, wise, and greatly devoted to God. He did everything he could to avoid getting caught up in any immorality.

The evil one called Satan had been observing Job. He then paid a visit to God, and God asked him to tell him where he had been.

"In places all over the earth," Satan bragged.

"Yes, you've been contriving, and I know you have been watching my righteous servant, Job."

"I have. He supposedly fears you, but for nothing you've protected him so well. He serves you only for what he receives from you. Take it all away, and he will deny you."

God answered, "Do what you will to all he owns, but you cannot touch Job himself."

Satan slunk away, determined to prove that Job would turn his back on God once he lost all that was precious to him. Suddenly chaos erupted. An army of Sabeans swept in, and violently stole Job's herds of oxen and donkeys. Lightning flashed and burned up thousands of sheep. Chaldeans attacked from three directions and took all the camels. A fierce wind riled across the desert, and destroyed the house of the eldest son where all of Job's children had gathered for a meal. The only survivors were four servants. They arrived one by one to report the devastation. The evil one likely watched and waited for the expected denial.

Overcome with distress, Job demonstrated his mourning through the prescribed and public rituals of his day. He tore his robe, then shaved his head. What he did next wasn't customary; it was personal. He fell to the ground and worshipped God.

For Job, the days ahead included much heart-searching. He faced friends who told him he got what he deserved. He wrestled with questions about the justice of God. In the end, Satan lost—Job did not turn his back on God.

Nothing in the universe can touch your life except by His permission and filtered through His fingers of love.

Kay Arthur

As quickly as a dish can crash to the floor, a peaceful day can turn to chaos. Job's devastation came swiftly. He wondered if God had brought on all the loss and suffering. Yet, instead of repelling who he believed caused it all, he worshipped him.

Without hesitation Job fell down and worshipped God. Having lost so much, he didn't want to lose God's presence. Job invites God to come closer in his time of sorrow. He was wise and humble enough to cling to God, not because he understood him, but because he trusted him. What a magnificent expression of an established intimate relationship.

His next words show that he had an honorable perspective of God—and his lost possessions. He knows he was born with nothing—no money, reputation, land, animals, or children. He acquired all his gifts from God. Job didn't realize Satan was the one who fiercely ripped them from his grasp, but he peacefully declared that God had the right to have done so.

By the time the poetic drama lowered its curtains, Job had a conversation with God. His understanding grew deeper, and he worshipped God even more.

> Alone. Naked before God. It's how He created us in the Garden, and it's the only way we can truly know Him—utterly bare, vulnerable, needy.
>
> Mesu Andrews

As they did with Job, the agonizing thoughts and raw emotions that accompany your pain can carry you to a place of unbelievable nearness to God. Refuse to let anything rob you of intimacy and closeness.

As Job stated each of his beliefs about God, his own words became a comfort. He would not resent or blame anyone. This perspective left him free to go to God in worship and praise, and then to begin to heal from the grief he felt from his loss.

Perhaps your loss has become entangled in regrets, resentment, and blame. Instead of tenaciously holding on to these, let them go so you are free to cling to God. Consider what you know about him, and form your own statements of comfort and praise. Trust that in time your understanding of the situation, and of God, will grow deeper. And, like Job, so will your desire and ability to worship God—even in the midst of your pain.

God is beautifully orchestrating the outcome of your loss—even while you don't see it. Having lost so much, don't lose his presence. He invites you to come yet closer.

Behold, we consider those blessed who remained stead-fast. You have heard of the steadfastness of Job, and you have seen the purpose of the Lord, how the Lord is compassionate and merciful.

James 5:11 ESV

Job learned that life is hard and often not fair. Harry Adams, in the *AMG Concise Bible Survey*, discussed what readers can learn from considering Job's responses to his loss:

"First we must dislodge the notion from our thinking that life should be fair because we are Christians. Faith does not come with a guarantee that says 'no more problems.' Second, we must not allow trials to turn us against God. Rather, they should make us cling all the more to him as we endure."

In *Job's Resignation*, Charles Spurgeon encouraged readers to work through sorrow by directing their devotion toward God:

"O dear friend, when thy grief presses thee to the very dust, worship there! ... That kind of worshipping which lies in the subduing of the will, the arousing of the affections, the bestirring of the whole mind and heart, and the presentation of oneself unto God over again in solemn consecration, must tend to sweeten sorrow, and to take the sting out of it."

Zooming **In**

The book of Job, though considered historically true, is a type of "dramatic" poetry. It is also "Wisdom Literature" because of the depth of its practical teaching. Other significant pieces of Wisdom Literature have been discovered with similar stories to Job, but with different perspectives. One, "A Dispute Over Suicide," was composed in Egypt around 2000 BC, and another, "Babylonian Theodicy," was written around 1000 BC. Both, like Job, have main characters struggling to understand their suffering. No one really knows when Job was written, but based on the names of places in the book, it is believed that the man Job might have lived around the time of Abraham.

Job considered that he had lost everything, and would truly despair if he had lost God's presence—the presence that comforts.

Through the
Eyes of
Your Heart

Deep losses are like shattered crystal—impossible to piece back together. Have you felt that? Share it here in a prayer to God.

_____

_____

_____

In his loss, Job clung to God. You can too, not because you understand, but because you trust. Let your pain take you nearer to God. What little steps of trust can you take?

_____

_____

_____

Statements of truth about who God is can be turned into lovely expressions of worship. They can bring comfort. What are some of those truths? Turn them into words of praise.

_____

_____

_____

_____

Open Hands

When Elijah came near the town gate of Zarephath, he saw a widow gathering sticks for a fire. "Would you please bring me a cup of water?" he asked. As she left to get it, he asked, "Would you also please bring me a piece of bread?"

1 Kings 17:10–11 CEV

The Big Picture

By God's direction, Elijah, the prophet, traveled west from his homeland. He visited King Ahab in Jezreel, but Ahab, and the wicked Queen Jezebel, despised the prophet for his admonitions to turn back to God. Elijah warned him there would be no rain, and a famine would come to the land. No surprise they became angry.

As Elijah fled the king, God led him to a brook near a place called Cherith. Here God hid Elijah and took care of him. For some time, Elijah stayed in this place. He drank water from the brook, and ravens miraculously brought food each morning and evening. There had been no rain, just as Elijah had said. When the brook dried up, God told Elijah to go to Zarephath. A widow there would help care for him. Indeed, as Elijah drew near the city gate of Zarephath, he found a woman gathering sticks. Perhaps she was the widow God spoke of.

"Please, could you bring me a little water to drink?" he asked her. With a weak nod, she turned to fetch the water. "And please, could you also bring me a piece of bread?" the prophet added.

"I tell you the truth," she answered, "as certain as Jehovah your God lives, I have nothing baked—only a small handful of flour and a saucer of oil. In fact, I was gathering sticks to build a fire to prepare the last meal for me and my son before we die."

Surely this wasn't who God intended? Elijah decided to see. "Don't fear that you will die. Take what you have to make a loaf. Bring it to me, and then make some for you and your son." She didn't seem shocked by the request. Elijah went on. "This is what the God of Israel says: 'your flour and oil will not run out until the day God sends rain to this place.'"

The widow believed Elijah, and did as he asked. She made the cakes, and the flour and oil supply never ran out—just as God had said. She fed herself, her son, and the prophet for many days. Through God's continual provision, both the prophet and the widow saw the steady faithfulness of God.

No matter how little you have, you can always give some of it away.

Catherine Marshall

Take a
Closer Look

So many needs—how do you keep your heart and hands open? Though the widow's own needs were great, she did not let that stop her from helping someone else. Her character and her trust in God were behind her kindhearted response.

Elijah didn't know for certain that this was the widow God meant to provide for him. Only the poor gathered sticks. What would she be able to do? God, faith . . . something made him ask her for food. Her response says much about her. It was a custom in ancient Phoenicia to give water to strangers, but her attitude shows that she did so graciously. She then was willing to offer Elijah food, but feared she may not have enough to satisfy him. When he assured her that God would provide, she believed without hesitation.

This in itself is amazing. The widow lived in a place famous for Baal worship—the same Phoenician religion that influenced Ahab and Jezebel's rebellion against God. Notice that when Elijah asked her for bread, she spoke of *his* God. She was a Phoenician, and yet she called Elijah's God by name. It was he who she trusted.

> *I will be kind to the poor, for they are alone. Kind to the rich, for they are afraid. And kind to the unkind, for such is how God has treated me.*
>
> Max Lucado

You open your home to friends and strangers. You feed others before you feed yourself. You are one of the first to make a meal for someone who has been ill. Caring for others, nurturing, and showing hospitality come naturally.

Apply It
to Your Life

Or maybe not. Instead, you might be saying, "I only wish I had the ability to do even one of those things well," "I wish I'd think to help someone in need," or "I have so little to share." You're not alone. Even those who seem to have more of a knack for being aware of and taking care of needs, struggle in one way or another. Simply be willing, and you will find that you are able to help others in need, regardless of your skill or how much you have in resources.

Remember the widow had just a few sticks, a handful of flour, and a tiny bit of oil. She barely had the energy to speak to Elijah. But a whispered yes was all that was needed, and God provided. When you say yes, when you share what you have, trust God to provide what is needed.

This is how we know what love is: Christ gave his life for us. We too, then, ought to give our lives for others!

1 John 3:16 GNT

How Others
See It

The widow, whom God brought to help Elijah, offered what little she had and got much more than she ever expected. Robert Jamieson, in the *Jamieson, Fausset, and Brown Commentary*, said this:

"Meeting, at his entrance into the town, the very woman who was appointed by divine providence to support him, his faith was severely tested by learning from her that her supplies were exhausted and that she was preparing her last meal for herself and son. . . . She received a prophet's reward, and for the one meal afforded to him, God, by a miraculous increase of the little stock, afforded many to her."

Before Elijah arrived, God planned for the widow to help him. Charles Spurgeon, in his sermon "The Widow at Sarepta," said:

"She had no idea of sustaining a man of God out of that all but empty barrel of meal! Yet the Lord, who never lies, spoke a solemn Truth when He said, 'I have commanded a widow woman there.' He had so operated on her mind that He had prepared her to obey the command when it did come by the lip of His servant the Prophet."

Zooming **In**

There is a Zarephath, New Jersey, but Elijah and the widow's Zarephath was a Phoenician seaport located between Tyre and Sidon. The Greeks called it Sarepta, and today it is a large village called Sarafend. *Zarephath* means "smelting shop"—a workshop where metals are melted and refined.

The ancient civilization of Phoenicia was located where Lebanon and Syria are today. Its location near the seacoast created a profitable sea trade business for its people. The Greek's word for *Phoenician, Phoinike,* was similar to "purple" or "crimson," and the people became famous for their dyed textiles. They were often known as the "Purple People."

The widow expected to die soon, not feed a prophet. But God sent him. How could she say no? How could she not trust? God sends opportunities every day. Do you see them?

Through the
Eyes of
Your Heart

It could be as simple as a request for a paper clip. Maybe a cup of tea. Just a moment of your time. Small needs. Simple requests. Look back a day or two. What opportunities did you have?

_____

_____

_____

What different perspective does the widow offer on "giving from the little you have"? What would that look like for you?

_____

_____

_____

"Yes." That little word is packed with grace, generosity, and faith. Just be willing. Think of a friend in need, and plan how you can surprise her with a burst of "yes!"

_____

_____

_____

All the Way

Jesus told them, "You don't know what you are asking! Are you able to drink from the bitter cup of sorrow I am about to drink?" "Oh yes," they replied, "we are able!" "You will indeed drink from it," he told them. "But I have no right to say who will sit on the thrones next to mine. My Father has prepared those places for the ones he has chosen."

Matthew 20:22–23 NLT

**The
Big Picture**

How costly are some dreams, some friendships . . . but oh, so worth it.

On their way to Jerusalem, Jesus pulled his twelve disciples aside from the others who traveled with him. "We're going to Jerusalem. What the prophets said about the Son of Man will happen," he warned them. "He will be beaten, mocked, and killed, but he will come alive again after three days." He spoke of himself, but his disciples didn't understand. They believed Jesus was bound to rule in Jerusalem as their king and conqueror. Perhaps they would rule with him.

Two in particular dreamed of their reign alongside Jesus—James and John. On one occasion, their mother, Salome, came with her sons to speak to Jesus. They approached him and kneeled. "We seek a favor, and ask that you not deny it," the mother said.

"What is it you want me to do?"

"Bid my two sons to sit at your side in your kingdom, one on your right, and one on your left," she requested.

Jesus directed his answer to James and John. "You do not understand what you are asking," he said. "Would you be able to handle even a little of what I'm about to endure?"

"We are able to," they told him.

"You are certain to, but as to who will sit on my right or left side, that is not my choice. God has already made this decision."

The news of James and John's request spread among the other ten, who became angry. They thought the two had received a special privilege, and they were frustrated they hadn't asked first.

Jesus saw this and said, "You've watched how rulers control those under them. It should be different with you. Those here who want to be the greatest should instead be your humble teachers and servants." Then he spoke of himself and said, "The Son of Man didn't come to be waited on, but to serve others—even to the point of giving his life so others could become free to live for God."

"To be great you must serve," was a paradox for these twelve men. They still did not fully understand the principles of Jesus' kind of kingdom. Up to the end of his life on earth, he showed them what it meant, and knew they would one day understand.

Life becomes harder for us when we live for others, but it also becomes richer and happier.

Albert Schweitzer

Maybe you've so bubbled over with desire for a goal that you lost track of the reality of what you hoped for. Notice how the disciples' grand vision for their future obscured any true understanding of it. They had no idea what it would cost to be by King Jesus' side.

God's picture is bigger and reaches far beyond anyone's immediate circumstances and life. Jesus tried to give part of the picture to the intimate Twelve, but they held tenaciously to their own: he was sent to save their nation, not to be beaten and killed . . . wasn't he?

Jesus asked James and John if they were able to drink from the cup he was about to drink from. *Cup,* or *poterion* in Greek, figuratively refers to "lot" or "fate." It was Jesus' place, and his only, to suffer and die to redeem mankind. But were the disciples willing to take even a sip of this suffering? James and John reply, "We are able to." At least they were willing, but they still didn't understand. They wouldn't be fighting a battle for a marble throne; they would suffer for something greater—faith in God to be passed on to generations for eternity.

> *God did not save you to be a sensation. He saved you to be a servant.*
>
> John E. Hunter

Take a moment to set aside your bills, your piles of laundry, your apron, or your briefcase. Yes, forget about those for a moment. Now dream a little. When you look past all the daily "have to's," think about what you wish for.

There's a bigger picture to all you envision happening in your life. Even what you might see as menial has an impact in the greater arena of the world and history. Young or old, small or great, you are a part of a beautiful, unfolding plan—God's plan. Your smallest act of service, when done wholeheartedly for him, ripples across the sea of humanity. Now that is something worth longing to be a part of.

Yes, the cost of serving in imitation of Jesus can be high. Jesus still holds out the cup he spoke of to John and James and asks you, his daughter, "Are you willing?" All you need is the willingness to go beyond the limits of your vision, beyond your own capability; he'll do the rest. Be his wholehearted friend. It's oh so worth it.

Ah Lord God! It is you who made the heavens and the earth by your great power and by your outstretched arm! Nothing is too hard for you.

Jeremiah 32:17 NRSV

Jesus used the image of a cup to refer to his imminent suffering, death, and sacrifice for mankind. Don Fortner, in his sermon "Five Great Things," addressed this:

"A cup is something taken voluntarily. The Lord of glory willingly took the cup of wrath when he was made to be sin for us. Voluntarily, with one tremendous draught of love, drank damnation dry for us! He so loved us that he took the cup of God's wrath as our Substitute as willingly as a thirsty man takes a cup of water!"

Jesus asked his disciples if they were willing to suffer with him. Dr. Ray Pritchard, in his sermon "The Mother of Twins: Christ Speaks to the Problem of Misguided Ambition," said:

"Here we come to the bottom line of life. Are you willing to sacrifice everything that is dear to you in order to follow Christ? If the answer is yes, then you can also share in the rewards. These are not words to toss around lightly. You only make this kind of commitment when you have found something worth giving your life for."

Zooming **In**

Sitting next to the king's throne was a sign of honor to the Jews. Egyptians, Romans, and Africans are also among the cultures that practiced this. To be on the right was more often considered greater than on the left; however, Cyrus, king of ancient Persia, put his guests to his left because it was nearest to his heart.

In Jewish and Greco-Roman cultures, elderly women held a place of respect not given to younger women. An older woman, like John and James's mother, could get away with making bold requests that even men couldn't make. It didn't mean that they would receive what they requested, but traditionally they were allowed to ask.

The disciples dreamed of thrones. What Jesus asked of them instead would be hard, but what he asked would have an impact they'd never regret. Get caught up in God's dream for you.

Through the
Eyes of
Your Heart

Be famous, be rich, be beautiful, be thin—oh, the pressures! It's hard to get away from them. What would Jesus tell you to "be" instead? Hint: It's much more rewarding.

_____

_____

_____

Kindness ripples and touches other lives. It's a little part of what God can do through you in the lives around you. Think of those you care about. What is one ripple you can start?

_____

_____

_____

If you painted a picture of your life, and the dreams you have for it, what would it look like? Now let God take you outside the limits of your canvas. What do you see?

_____

_____

_____

_____

Please, God, Would You?

The Big Picture

It was Thursday during the Passover festivities. The Jews were commemorating the historical event of when God had saved their nation from death while in Egypt. For those with Jesus, the night of celebration would be filled with quivering unease, but also words of promise and peace.

Jesus gathered his twelve disciples into a room, in the upper part of a home where they were staying in Jerusalem. He knew what the next day held. It would be the pinnacle of his mission, but extremely difficult for him— and for his disciples.

Earlier in the evening he had laid aside his robes and washed their feet. Jesus, servant to mankind, God in the flesh, would soon give his life and offer a deeper washing—a soul cleansing. As they talked and ate the Passover supper together, he warned them that he would be betrayed by one of them. He told them this to show that as God in the flesh, he knew these things.

"What is about to happen to me is to glorify God. I won't be with you much longer." He went on. "I give you a new life-rule to follow: Love each other. I have shown you how. Others will see this and know you have learned from me."

"Where are you going?" Peter asked. "I'd follow you anywhere. I'd die for you."

"You would? Before you hear a rooster crowing in the morning, you will turn your back on me three times." He turned and offered words of assurance. "Believe by what I've said and done, the Father and I are one. You've seen me; you've seen him. You'll do works like I've done and even greater." With barely a breath he went on. "Ask whatever you want in my name, and I will do it, so God can be glorified in me. Anything. I will do it."

Deep into the night Jesus tenderly shared his love and comfort for what was to come. Hours passed as powerful, eternal words were spoken. Then together, all except Judas Iscariot, who had left during the meal, they traveled across the Kidron Valley to a garden. That dark Friday Jesus would be betrayed and led to his death, but with the promise that he would soon be raised to life—and to give life.

I can testify, with a full and often wonder-stricken awe, that I believe God answers prayer. I know God answers prayer!

Mary Slessor

Nothing beats a great friend—another woman who understands you, and encourages you to share your heart. But have any of your friends ever told you, "Ask whatever you want—just use my name—and you've got it." Jesus said something like that, and many now pray for whatever they want. Often overlooked, however, is how to ask, and the reason why God would answer.

Jesus offers a promise in John 14:13. The promise began with "whatever you ask." *Ask, aiteo* in Greek, means "beg," "desire," "crave," or "require." Sounds pretty wide open. But then Jesus added, "In My name." To pray in his name is to pray out of intimate communion with Jesus—from a daily relationship that acknowledges who he is as God, that acknowledges all he has done for you through the sacrifice of his life on the cross.

Then he says there is a reason for such a prayer: so that "the Father may be glorified in the Son." Your prayers of request become an expression of your worship of God, and express your unity with him. They shed a wondrous light on who he is for others to see.

> *The purpose of prayer is to find God's will and to make that will our prayer.*
>
> Catherine Marshall

You know your friend is available. She told you to call anytime. And yet sometimes you don't. It's a risk to pick up the phone and call, to expose the feelings and thoughts that reveal who you really are.

At times it can feel that way—even with God. You know he's there. You know he knows all the details, and most of the time you really believe he cares. But talk to him about it? It seems easier to push through on your own than to face him.

When that happens, consider involving one of your praying friends. Call and ask her to pray with you, to help you bend your heart toward God in worship, and to release your need into his caring hands. Move closer to him in your prayers. Trust that he has your good in mind—whatever the answer.

When Jesus invited his disciples to pray in his name and ask for anything, he was inviting them into an intimate relationship with God. His invitation extends to you, too. He's available anytime, longing for you to know him well.

If you abide in Me, and My words abide in you, ask whatever you wish, and it will be done for you.

John 15:7 NASB

God delights in his children seeking him out in moments of need. Rosalind Goforth, in *How I Know . . . God Answers Prayer*, spoke about prayer within the special relationship between you and God:

"Prayer has been hedged about with too many man-made rules. I am convinced that God has intended prayer to be as simple and natural and as constant a part of our spiritual life as the relationship between a child and his parent in the home. And as a large part of that relationship between child and parent is simply asking and receiving, just so is it with us and our heavenly Parent."

You can ask what you want in the name of Jesus, and he will do it. Leon Morris, in his commentary, *The New International Commentary on the New Testament: The Gospel According to John,* explained:

"This does not mean simply using the name as a formula. It means that prayer is to be in accordance with all that the name stands for. It is prayer proceeding from faith in Christ, prayer that gives expression to a unity with all that Christ stands for, prayer which seeks to set forward Christ Himself."

Zooming In

The room where Jesus and his twelve disciples gathered was called the Upper Room. It is also called the *Cenacle,* from the Latin *cena,* meaning "dinner." The supposed site survived the destruction of Jerusalem in AD 70, and so became the meeting place for the first Christian church. It was destroyed twice, first by Persians, and later by Muslims. The second time, the Crusaders replaced it with a basilica. From 1333 to 1552, it was cared for by Franciscan monks. Jerusalem was then captured by Turks, and the Cenacle became a mosque. Christians returned when Israel was established as a state in 1948. Today the Cenacle is owned by the Catholic Church.

> *"I'm getting ready to leave. You won't see me anymore, but I won't be far away," Jesus was telling his disciples. "Let's stay close. When you need something, ask."*

Do you have too many emotions whirling inside? When you do, it's hard to share with your best friend, or even with God. Try writing them down and turn them into a letter to God.

What beautiful love Jesus had for his disciples. He has it for you, too. He's inviting you to come close, be vulnerable, feel safe. What do you want to ask him for? Thank him for?

You're lovely—a wonderful, walking reflection of God, especially when he has answered prayer through you. What answers to prayers do you see within your life?

Put It on Me

When Abigail saw David, she hurried and got down from the donkey and fell before David on her face and bowed to the ground. She fell at his feet and said, "On me alone, my lord, be the guilt. Please let your servant speak in your ears, and hear the words of your servant."

1 Samuel 25:23–24 ESV

Oh, the influence of a wise woman.

The Big Picture

A rich Israelite man named Nabal lived in Paran with his wife, Abagail. Nabal means "foolish," and as you'll see, that's exactly how this man behaved. He was considered cruel and devious in his dealings. He had three thousand sheep, plus a thousand goats. It was sheepshearing time for Nabal and his men. In celebration, they would hold a great feast.

During this time, Saul still reigned over Israel, but was jealous of David and sought to kill him. David escaped to the wilderness with six hundred men, and ended up in Paran near Nabal's herds.

When David heard that Nabal was shearing his sheep and about to have a feast, he asked ten young men to go greet the sheep owner on his behalf. He hoped to receive Nabal's favor and food for his men.

Nabal likely knew who David was, including that he had been anointed king by Samuel the prophet, but he responded, "Why should I give my hard-earned food to these lowlife scoundrels?"

When David heard Nabal's reply, his anger sparked into fury. He gathered two-thirds of his men, and told them to destroy Nabal and all he owned.

At the same time, one of Nabal's men reported to Abigail how her husband had treated David's men. "The men never hurt us or stole from us. In fact, they protected us. Consider how you will respond," he told Abigail, "for we are in danger for what our master has done."

Abigail quickly gathered a feast to present to David and all his men, and had it loaded on donkeys. "Go ahead of me," she told her servants. "I will come after you." She kept this secret from her husband.

When she saw David approaching, she quickly dismounted her donkey and bowed to the ground. "Let me take the guilt for my husband's foolish deed. Please hear what I have to say."

Over the next moments, Abigail gently and humbly spoke to David to calm his anger. "God has kept you from shedding blood that you would regret." She presented the gifts of food, and begged his forgiveness, then said, "He is preparing you to rule well and without a reputation of evil. Remember me, your servant, when God has helped you succeed."

David's anger quieted, and he thanked God for sending Abigail to stop him. He realized how close he had come to responding rashly because of unchecked anger.

A gentle answer turns away anger,
but a harsh word stirs up wrath.

Proverbs 15:1 HCSB

What incredible opportunities women have to be graceful and creative peacemakers. Abigail was that kind of woman. She humbled herself before David and took Nabal's folly as her own. Isn't that so like what Jesus did when he came to live on earth as a human, and then died on the cross for the follies of all?

Abigail lowered herself before David, but she did so with great dignity and wisdom. Every detail of her plan, every word she spoke, was carefully thought out to bring peace and restoration to a situation headed toward destruction and death. She didn't know if it would work, but it was worth the risk, even if it meant her own death.

Abigail requested that the guilt of her husband's act be transferred to her. *Avon,* the Hebrew word for "guilt," also means "evil," "punishment," and "sin." Her husband had been foolish, but she accepted the responsibility, and any consequences, to save him.

Abigail didn't know it, but God planned the ultimate substitution in his Son, Jesus. A thousand years later Jesus humbly bowed before a heated crowd who shouted "Guilty!" at his utter innocence. He took on the fault and the punishment for the follies of all humankind—those done long ago, today, and tomorrow.

> *A woman is like a tea bag. You never know her strength until you drop her in hot water.*
>
> Nancy Reagan

The Bible encourages women to have a gentle and quiet spirit. Put that in the context of Abigail's actions, and you see that a humble and submissive spirit can be one that is lined with silk, with dignity and strength, able to smooth relationships, creatively and wisely.

Apply It
to Your Life

Life is full of conflict and misunderstanding, just as much now as in Abigail's time. It looks a bit different, but some of the principles are the same. Abigail considered what she needed to do, then prepared and acted quickly. She didn't wait until after the disaster, but worked to avert it.

She considered what she needed to do to present her good intention, and chose to send gifts. Today a kind note might be exactly what's needed. Abigail then took responsibility for the problem. She didn't say it was her fault, but neither did she blame David. Then she helped David see God's perspective and the future if he chose a good path. She negotiated calmly, and brought peace to the situation.

When those around you are making harmful choices that affect you and those you love, like Abigail, you can seek to gently and wisely work toward resolution.

Blessed are those who make peace. They will be called God's children.

Matthew 5:9 GOD'S WORD

Robert H. Roe, in his sermon "David and Abigail, Part II," shared how Abigail wisely helped David regain a sound perspective of his situation:

"See how you win an argument with a willful, rebellious, unrepentant, angry man? You point him to the Lord and take the humble place. You get yourself out of the argument and get it between him and his God, instead of you and him with God somewhere around the periphery. That is all she did."

Thanks to Abigail, David was able to calm down and consider God's place in his situation. David H. Roper, in his sermon "David and Abigail," said:

"David needed to learn how to restrain himself in situations such as this, and Abigail came at a time when her ministry in his life was needed. She taught him, but she did it in a spirit of gentleness and quietness. . . . Her ministry was to get David's eyes on the Lord—off himself and his own anger and his own resources, and onto the Lord, who would take care of him."

Zooming **In**

Today donkeys are often seen as a symbol of stubbornness or stupidity, but historically they've also symbolized peace and humility. In ancient cultures, kings communicated their intentions by what beast they.rode. If they were going to war, they rode a horse. If they were seeking peace, they rode a donkey.

Early Israelites gave gifts for many reasons: to encourage the recipient to be gracious, to appease anger, to strengthen friendships, and to gain access into palaces. When treaties were signed, kings sent gifts to each other. Jewish law forbade the giving of gifts as a bribe to officers of justice.

Abigail took the responsibility for her husband's actions, but maintained integrity. God can help you wisely bring peace and calm to an out-of-control situation.

You, as a woman, have the opportunity to soften the hard edges of a difficult conflict with gentleness and wisdom. Do you have a situation like that right now? Describe it.

_____

_____

_____

With humility and creativity you can help those involved gain a clearer perspective. What do you see that they are having difficulty grasping because of their heated emotions?

_____

_____

_____

You might be taking a risk that has consequences for you. Pray and weigh it out, then act carefully. What steps, like Abigail's, can you take to bring resolution?

_____

_____

_____

_____

A Test of Love

God tested Abraham's faith and obedience. "Abraham!" God called. "Yes," he replied. "Here I am." "Take your son, your only son—yes, Isaac, whom you love so much—and go to the land of Moriah. Sacrifice him there as a burnt offering on one of the mountains, which I will point out to you."

Genesis 22:1–2 NLT

The Big Picture

A baby! Finally, a baby!

Just as God had said, Sarah and Abraham had a child. They were both well past childbearing age, even by the standards of their day. Abraham was a hundred years old, Sarah ninety. But they had a boy whom they named Isaac. What a delight he was—the beginning of a fulfilled promise. God had told them they would have an offspring who would launch a nation.

One day God spoke to Abraham. "Go fetch Sarah's and your son, Isaac, the one you love. Go to Moriah. You will offer him as a burnt offering on a mountain that I will direct you to."

Not a word from Abraham. Not one protest. But, oh, what must have been rumbling around in the heart of this father. The next morning Abraham rose, prepared his donkey, and split some wood. Two young men went with him and Isaac. Together the four traveled to Moriah. Three days later, Abraham saw the mountain in the distance that God told him about. "Rest here with

take a CLOSER look for women

the donkey," he told the men. "I'll go with my son and worship, and we'll both return to you." Surely God would make that possible, though Abraham didn't know how. He loved Isaac. Besides, didn't God promise that this boy would begin a nation?

Abraham loaded wood across his son's shoulders. He carried the fire starter and his knife. Together they began to walk to the top of the mountain.

"Father?"

"Yes, Isaac."

"We have the fire and the wood, but no lamb for the offering. Where's the lamb?"

"God will provide it, my son." How he hoped for that miracle. What did God have in mind?

They arrived at the right place. Abraham built the altar, and set the wood in place. Quietly he bound his son and put him on the altar. He raised the knife—

"Abraham! Abraham! Don't touch the boy," said God in the form of an angel. "Through your willingness to give your only son for me, you have shown that you trust me."

A rustling noise came from a nearby bush, and Abraham found a ram tangled by its horns. He untied the boy, and gave the ram as the offering instead of his son. Abraham named this memorable place *Jehovah-Jireh*, which means "God has seen and provided."

> *What seems too difficult for us is a sure sign*
> *that it belongs to God.*
>
> Marie Depree

Oh, the fear of hearing words that seem to shatter a vow—your security shaken. God asked Abraham to give up his son, even sacrifice him. But notice. Abraham's ability to climb to the top of that mountain rested in his belief that God would not go against his own word.

God had given Abraham the promise that his descendants would be as numerous as the stars. Abraham believed him. In spite of his age, he would have a son and many descendants. Then God spoke again. He asked that Abraham offer his beloved son as a sacrifice. Had God changed his mind? Abraham's faith would be tested, his obedience tried.

Abraham did well. He told his companions, "*We* will return," then gathered the supplies, and climbed the mountain with his son. He raised his knife, and only then did God stop him. The God who keeps his word is also Jehovah-Jireh, the God who provides.

God's test was meant to encourage and strengthen Abraham. What he required of Abraham he would one day require of himself, but the next time *the* Son would be sacrificed— God's beloved Son. His sacrifice fulfilled a promise of reconciliation between God and man. And God keeps his word.

> *Never be afraid to trust an unknown future to a known God.*
>
> Corrie ten Boom

God could never break one of his promises. But people do—all the time. And it hurts. How we respond to these hurts and broken promises reveals the depth of our faith. Will we continue climbing the mountain of life in full trust?

If you find you're holding on too tightly to a broken promise, it might be time to let go of all the security it seemed to offer, and of all the expectations that went with it. Living day after day, in the shadow of lost promises, prevents you from living the full life God has for you. Ask him to bring healing to your heart, and catch a glimpse of his vision for your life.

Remember that in Abraham's story God was not only a God who keeps his word, but he was also Jehovah-Jireh—the God who provides. Not only for Abraham, and not only for his son, but also for you. He gives life, and fullness, and promise beyond anything you can imagine, beyond anything any person can offer you.

In order to take what God has for you into your hands, you first have to let go of the lost promises. Let go and open your hands wide.

Trust in the LORD with all your heart, and do not lean on your own understanding. In all your ways acknowledge him, and he will make straight your paths.

Proverbs 3:5–6 ESV

Difficulties often draw out the question "Why?" George Whitefield, in *Abraham's Offering Up His Son Isaac,* addressed this:

"Your heart cries out, 'Why? Why should this happen to me?' Well, this is life's hardest trial. It is never so difficult when we can see a reason. However, when something happens to us in which we fail to see any logic, and in fact, everything seems to be against it, this is when faith is really put to the test."

For Abraham the question was about the promise God made. David Guzik, in his Enduring Word Commentary series, said:

"Abraham had to learn the difference between trusting the promise and trusting the Promiser. We can put God's promise before God Himself and feel it is our responsibility to bring the promise to pass, even if we have to disobey God to do it. . . . Trust the Promiser no matter what, and the promise will be taken care of!"

Zooming **In**

Mount Moriah, where God provided a substitute offering for Abraham, has great significance for different faiths. Later King David, after being instructed by the prophet Gad, purchased a site on Mount Moriah for the future temple of God. His son, King Solomon, eventually built the temple, a sacred place where the Jews worshipped God and offered sacrifices for their wrongdoings. Two thousand years after Abraham, Mount Moriah became the location where Jesus was crucified as a substitute offering for all of mankind. If you visit the area today, you'll find a Muslim mosque called the Dome of the Rock, built as a memorial to Abraham's journey with his son to the mountain.

When he asked Abraham to sacrifice his son, God hadn't broken his promise or even changed it. Do you need to believe someone's word? God's is trustworthy.

Through the
Eyes of
Your Heart

Promises and vows feel secure. When they are broken, you stop trusting—even God. Know he'd never betray you. What broken promises have hurt you? Tell him.

_____

_____

_____

Abraham believed God. He really did. But this request to sacrifice his son tested his faith and obedience to the limits. How have you felt your faith and obedience tested?

_____

_____

_____

Feeling tested? Struggling through a broken promise? God's design is for you to be strengthened like a refined diamond. In what ways do you see that already? What do you hope for?

_____

_____

_____

It's Foreign to Me

One of them, seeing that he was healed, returned and, with a loud voice, gave glory to God. He fell facedown at His feet, thanking Him. And he was a Samaritan. Then Jesus said, "Were not 10 cleansed? Where are the nine? Didn't any return to give glory to God except this foreigner?"

Luke 17:15–18 HCSB

The Big Picture

Jesus traveled quietly toward Jerusalem, far out of the clutches of those who sought his death. Many of the Jewish religious leaders feared he was winning the hearts of the people. This would be a political disaster. If they accepted him as their king—the long-awaited Messiah—the Romans who were in power might react by destroying Israel, perhaps even their temple.

Jesus was the Messiah, but he did not intend to rule as an earthly king. Yes, he was going to Jerusalem knowing he would be captured and put to death, but he also knew that he would be raised to life to reign on a heavenly throne. In the meantime, he had more to do. The road he traveled passed between Galilee and Samaria, two lands with people who despised each other—the Jews and the Samaritans.

In one village, a group of men stood off the road. They seemed to be watching for Jesus' arrival, but didn't dare come closer. They had leprosy, an infectious disease, which, by Jewish law, labeled them "unclean." They could go near no one. Nine of these leprous men were Jews; one was a foreigner—a Samaritan.

take a CLOSER look for women

"Jesus!" they called. "We know you can heal. Have compassion. Cleanse us from our leprosy."

Jesus saw them and said, "Go on. Present yourselves to the priests." Jewish law required that a priest declare lepers free of leprosy or "clean," but healing rarely occurred. The ten lepers knew this, and though they were still covered in sores, tumors, and deformities, in faith they obeyed Jesus.

How many steps the men took before the leprosy disappeared is not known, but all ten were healed. Nine rushed forward to the priests; one turned back to Jesus. In overflowing thanks, this one shouted praises to God, and fell to his face in front of Jesus' feet.

"Weren't ten of you healed?" Jesus asked. "Where are the others? So none returned to give God honor except this one foreigner?"

In gratefulness, the healed man stayed bowed at Jesus' feet. "Stand up," Jesus told him. "Go home to your family and friends. Because you have shown confidence in God, you are fully healed."

The man understood the wonder of his healing—and that God had done it. In the presence of this genuine outpouring of faith, Jesus healed the leper, body and soul.

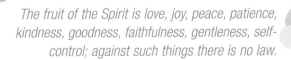

The fruit of the Spirit is love, joy, peace, patience, kindness, goodness, faithfulness, gentleness, self-control; against such things there is no law.

Galatians 5:22–23 ESV

What beautiful lessons can be learned by observing women of other cultures living out their faith in Jesus. For now, look more closely at this story. Notice which of the ten lepers expressed unreserved and genuine gratitude for his healing—the one considered a foreigner.

The Jews carried strong historical prejudices that blinded them from seeing any good in a Samaritan. In their eyes, these foreigners were coarse heathens who could be neither spiritual nor gracious. And yet it is the foreigner, not the nine Jews, who returns to thank Jesus.

What a beautiful dance of praise and faith the Samaritan expresses. He returns to give words of honor toward God. He does not hide his thankfulness for what he sees as undeserved compassion. He declares it with a "strong voice"—*megas phone* in Greek. He then falls to the ground and bows at Jesus' feet, recognizing him as God.

None of the ten earned the compassion given them, but it was the Samaritan who realized the depth of God's kindness, and poured out uninhibited gratefulness to Jesus. If the others had watched this one, perhaps their hearts might have softened toward those whom they had always despised.

> *Lord, you have given so much to me. Give me one thing more—a grateful heart.*
>
> George Herbert

Perhaps you have watched women of different faiths in America or other places in the world and have seen graces you wish were found in the Christianity you're familiar with. Without fear of compromising your own values, you can learn from these women. They could very well be displaying what Jesus taught.

Watch as they care for their families, love those in their communities, or integrate their faith into every facet of their lives. See how they creatively enjoy their femininity and express their beliefs in their homes, arts, and businesses. The American Indian woman, for instance, has been crafting pottery for over two thousand years. For each vessel she creates, she carries on the history, tradition, spiritual beliefs, and beauty of her culture—with dedication and grace.

Look for ways to draw from the experiences of other women—to integrate your faith and culture beautifully and graciously into all areas of your life, to love those who believe differently than you do, and to be more like Jesus. What better way could there be to honor God, and unreservedly thank him for all he's done for you?

Love your neighbor as yourself.
Matthew 22:39 NLT

The Bible story shows that the one who came back was the foreigner. Ray Pritchard, in his sermon "Where are the Nine?" said:

"When Luke adds, 'He was a Samaritan,' the shock is such that we ought to read it this way: 'Think of it. A Samaritan.'

"Remember, Jesus was a Jew, and the Jews thought Samaritans were half-breed traitors. To make matters worse, he is a Samaritan leper. To a Jew, a more repulsive combination could not be found. He was from the wrong race, he had the wrong religion, and he had the worst-possible disease.

"In religious matters, this Samaritan knew almost nothing, and what he knew was mostly wrong! But he knew Jesus had healed him, and he knew enough to be grateful to God. That statement is why this story is in the Bible. . . . What this story really means is that those who should have been most grateful weren't. And the one man who shouldn't have come back did."

Zooming In

In ancient times, leprosy was a highly contagious and devastating disease. No cure was known. Lesions formed, tissue disintegrated, limbs grew deformed, and nerve endings deadened. Even internal organs were affected. When the nerve endings were destroyed, the person lost feeling. Severe injury could occur, and the person may not even notice. Leprosy has come to be known as Hansen's disease, named after a Norwegian doctor who discovered the cause of the disease in 1873. Today it is under control in most of the world, but can still be a problem in countries like Brazil, India, Central Africa, and Tanzania.

The Samaritan leper was an outcast on two accounts—his disease and his heritage. But he was the one who beautifully thanked Jesus. That happens today, too.

Look around at other women who believe as you do, but who live or worship differently. What do you learn? Without compromising your values, what ways can you change?

_____

_____

_____

Enjoy talking to women of other faiths. Ask questions. What beautiful ways do they integrate their faith into their lifestyle? How can you do that with your faith?

_____

_____

_____

_____

As you watch other women, have you discovered any blind spots that keep you from loving them? What ways can you soften your heart toward others and love as Jesus loved?

_____

_____

_____

Courage to Count

If you persist in staying silent at a time like this, help and deliverance will arrive for the Jews from some-place else; but you and your family will be wiped out. Who knows? Maybe you were made queen for just such a time as this.

Esther 4:14 MSG

The Big Picture

It was a time of kings and queens, war and treachery. Judah was in captivity under the Persians, and in the midst of it all, a young Jewish girl was orphaned. Her name was Hadassah, or Esther. She was raised by her cousin Mordecai, and grew to be a beautiful young woman.

The Persian king Ahasuerus desired to show off the splendor of his kingdom, and so he held a 187-day banquet in his winter palace. During the last week of the feast, while drunk, he ordered Queen Vashti to appear in her royal crown. She refused. This angered the king, and by the advice of his trusted advisers, she was banished from the king's presence. Later his advisers encouraged him to search for a new queen among his 127 provinces. Young Esther was one of the many women prepared to appear before the king. He became captivated by her beauty and poise, and made her his new queen.

Mordecai advised Esther not to reveal her Jewish roots, and it wasn't widely known that he was her relative. Mordecai stayed near the palace to inquire after her well-being. During those years, the king made a man named Haman his chief officer, above all princes, and commanded that people bow when he passed. Mordecai always refused, telling those around him that he was a Jew. Haman became enraged. He convinced the king to send letters to the provinces issuing orders to kill all Jews on a certain day.

Mordecai grieved over this. He sent a message to Esther: "An order has been sent by the king to kill all Jews. Haman has offered to pay for their slaughter. You must approach the king and plead for your people."

Esther read the message, but it was against the law, and at risk of death, to approach the king without his summons. He had not called for her in thirty days. She sent a message back to Mordecai.

Mordecai replied, "You are not safe just because you are in the palace. If you remain silent, freedom will come another way for us, but consider this: maybe you are queen for this very reason—to save your people."

Queen Esther requested that all Jews fast for three days. After this, she carried out a bold plan to speak to the king and, through two specially prepared banquets for him and Haman, reveal the evil intent against her and the Jews. Esther risked her life and courageously saved her people.

Each of us may be sure that if God sends us on stony paths,
He will provide us with strong shoes, and He will not send us
out on any journey for which He does not equip us well.

Alexander MacLaren

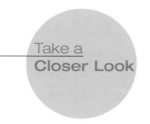

Yes, she was a woman shrouded in a foreign culture's cautions and laws, but Esther took a risk for her people. Notice that Mordecai tells Esther her rise to be queen might have been for "such a time as this." That simple statement points to a hand behind the events—God's.

At the time of Esther's reign, all Jews were in captivity under Persia. If Haman was successful, the Hebrew race would have been wiped out. God prevented that, and he began by preparing and positioning a little orphan girl to become a queen.

Her names were Hadassah and Esther. *Hadassah* comes from the Hebrew word *hadas,* which is a myrtle. Its leaves release a full fragrance when they are bruised and crushed. Likewise, Hadassah's purpose was brought to fullness through difficulties. Though *Esther* means "star," it is related to the word *hester,* meaning "hidden." The queen courageously revealed her hidden ancestry when it would save her and her nation.

Mordecai believed in God's providence behind all the events of Esther's life, and challenged her to rise up to her purpose. Each event prepared her to be in the right position to deliver her people, the Jews.

> *Expect great things from God;*
> *attempt great things for God.*
>
> William Carey

Esther was not a robot, destined to be a certain kind of person for a particular purpose. God does not work that way. The little girl growing into a woman had choices to make along the way. Perhaps it was partly the wise guardianship of Mordecai, that helped Esther grow into a woman not only of beauty, but, more important, a woman

Apply It
to Your Life

of character. She was true to her faith, and possessed a sensitive and courageous heart.

When the time came, she used the resources God gave her, personally and as a woman. In all her femininity, she fought for the lives of her Hebrew nation—no matter how controversial it was, no matter how far out of reach the goal seemed. Yes, softheartedness and femininity, wisely used and guided by God's Spirit, can be used to fiercely fight evil.

Purpose and preparation are very much a part of what God has in mind for those who trust and live for him. God is working in the world, and in your life, just as he did in Esther's. Though he may not put you in a position to become a queen and save a nation, his purposes for your life are just as important. Meet those with courage.

Wait for the LORD; be strong and let your heart take courage; yes, wait for the LORD.

Psalm 27:14 NASB

Though God is not mentioned in the book of Esther, he is not absent in the events. Dr. Harry Adams, in *The AMG Concise Bible Survey,* believed God was clearly working behind the scenes. He said:

"He is as hidden in the book as he can be in life. Yet God's hand is obviously at work. . . . What is a crisis to us is no crisis to God. Neither people nor events can thwart his plans. Therefore, when we encounter evil, we must act boldly while trusting mightily in his unseen presence and ongoing providence."

Mordecai believed his cousin could courageously be a part of the deliverance of all the Jews. In his Enduring Word Commentary series, David Guzik said:

"Mordecai knows that God has promoted this orphan in exile for a reason—and Esther must have the courage and wisdom to see that reason and walk in it. . . . This principle applies very much to us as well; God promotes us or puts [us] in a place for a reason, and we need the courage and wisdom to see that reason and to walk in it."

Zooming **In**

Today Purim is one of the favorite of Jewish holidays. It is a commemoration of when the Jewish people, living in Persia, were saved from annihilation through Queen Esther's actions. The festival is celebrated on the fourteenth day of Adar, or March, because it was the thirteenth day of Adar when Haman had planned to murder all Jews.

The Common myrtle, or *Myrtus communis* in Latin, is an evergreen shrub found most often in the Mediterranean. If you hold its leaves to the light, you will see many tiny, translucent pockets of fragrance. The sweet scent is released by crushing the leaves.

To her people, Esther truly was like a fragrance released through crushing. They were saved by her courage to do what she felt God required of her.

There are so many qualities of a woman besides what you see in Esther. What do you see as your "queenly" strengths? How are you using them?

_____

_____

_____

_____

Preparation leads to purpose, character to courage. It's an ongoing process. In what ways are you still becoming a woman of character? What would you like to work on?

_____

_____

_____

All of who you are as a woman, when guided by God's Spirit, will help you rise to your purpose and have the courage to count. How do you see God's hand behind his purpose for you?

_____

_____

_____

Hudson Taylor

I have found that there are three stages in every great work of God: first, it is impossible, then it is difficult, then it is done.

*What is impossible with
men is possible with God.*

Luke 18:27 NIV

Dennis Covington

Mystery is not the absence of meaning, but the presence of more meaning than we can comprehend.

Look up at the sky! Who created the stars you see? The one who leads them out like an army, he knows how many there are and calls each one by name! His power is so great—not one of them is ever missing!

Isaiah 40:26 GNT

C. S. Lewis

We trust not because a god exists, but because this God exists.

I'm not saying that I have this all together, that I have it made. But I am well on my way, reaching out for Christ, who has so wondrously reached out for me.

Philippians 3:12 MSG